WORKING WI

Suffolk

How To Books on Jobs & Careers

Applying for a Job
Becoming an Au Pair
Career Networking
Career Planning for Women
Doing Voluntary Work Abroad
Finding a Job in Canada
Finding a Job in Computers
Finding a Job with a Future
Finding Work Overseas
Freelance DJ-ing
Freelance Teaching & Tutoring
Getting into Films & TV
Getting That Job
Getting Your First Job
How to Be a Freelance Journalist
How to Be a Freelance Sales Agent
How to Be a Freelance Secretary
How to Find Temporary Work Abroad
How to Get a Job Abroad
How to Get a Job in Hotels & Catering
How to Get a Job in America
How to Get a Job in Australia
How to Get a Job in Europe
How to Get a Job in France
How to Get a Job in Germany

How to Get into Radio
How to Get That Job
How to Know Your Rights at Work
How to Manage Your Career
How to Market Yourself
How to Return to Work
How to Start a New Career
How to Work from Home
How to Work in an Office
How to Work in Retail
How to Work with Dogs
Learning New Job Skills
Living & Working in China
Passing that Interview
Surviving Redundancy
Working as a Holiday Rep
Working in Japan
Working in Photography
Working in Travel & Tourism
Working on Contract Worldwide
Working on Cruise Ships
Working with Children
Working with Horses
Writing a CV that Works

Other titles in preparation

The How To series now contains more than 200 titles in the following categories:

Business Basics
Family Reference
Jobs & Careers
Living & Working Abroad
Media Skills

Mind & Body
New Technology
Student Handbooks
Successful Writing
Travel

Please send for a free copy of the latest catalogue for full details (see back cover for address).

JOBS & CAREERS

WORKING WITH CHILDREN

How to find the right qualifications, training and job opportunities

Meg Jones

Cartoons by Mike Flanagan

British Library Cataloguing-in-Publication data
A catalogue record for this book is available from the British Library.

© Copyright 1997 by Meg Jones.

First published in 1997 by How To Books Ltd, 3 Newtec Place,
Magdalen Road, Oxford OX4 1RE, United Kingdom.
Tel: (01865) 793806. Fax: (01865) 248780.

All rights reserved. No part of this work may be reproduced, or stored in
an information retrieval system (other than for purposes of review),
without the express permission of the Publisher in writing.

Note: The material contained in this book is set out in good faith for
general guidance and no liability can be accepted for loss or expense
incurred as a result of relying in particular circumstances on statements
made in the book. The laws and regulations are complex and liable to
change, and readers should check the current position with the relevant
authorities before making personal arrangements.

Produced for How To Books by Deer Park Productions.
Typeset by Kestrel Data, Exeter.
Printed and bound in Great Britain by
Cromwell Press, Broughton Gifford, Melksham, Wiltshire.

Contents

List of illustrations	8
Preface	9

1 Working with young children — 13

Considering your options	13
Weighing up the qualities required	15
Transferring your skills	18
Coping with your own children	20
Case study	22
Considering the financial implications	23
Discussion points	25

2 Gaining experience — 26

Looking for the openings	26
Case study	27
Looking for established groups	28
Using your special interests	33
Discussion points	36

3 Working with babies and the under fives — 37

Undertaking group care	37
Opting for family care	40
Case study	41
Focusing on specialist care	43
Going into selective care	46
Discussion points	46

4	**Working with older children**	47
	Running a play session	47
	Case study	50
	Holidaying with pay	53
	Teaching	55
	Discussion points	55
5	**Searching for other initiatives**	57
	Setting up a shoppers' creche	57
	Promoting child friendly cities	58
	Keeping fit	60
	Case study	60
	Organising childcare at special events	62
	Discussion points	67
6	**Training and qualifying**	68
	Seeking advice	68
	Choosing a course	69
	Attending training	75
	Case study	76
	Assessing the alternatives	76
	Discussion points	80
7	**Preparing for the job market**	81
	Collecting for a portfolio	81
	Finding out about jobs	81
	Reading the advertisement	84
	Case study	86
	Writing the letter of application	87
	Applying for the job	90
	Discussion points	94
8	**Getting through the interview**	96
	Preparing for the big day	96
	Knowing what to expect	98
	Being ready for the questions	100
	Case study	101
	What happens next	102

	Seeking advice or counselling	103
	Discussion points	104
9	**Getting the best out of the job**	105
	Learning from others	105
	Developing relationships	106
	Practising your skills	108
	Case study	108
	Taking advantage of in-service training	109
	Seeking further training	110
	Discussion points	112
10	**Moving on**	113
	Being alert to further opportunities	113
	Travelling the hierarchy	116
	Case study	117
	Developmental training	118
	Discussion points	120

Appendix: National Vocational Qualifications Standards	121
Glossary	127
Further reading	129
Useful addresses	131
Index	138

List of Illustrations

1. Listing your attributes — 16
2. Attribute self-assessment form — 17
3. Personal assessment form — 19
4. Variety of work with children — 29
5. Acceptable/unacceptable words — 31
6. Ideas for themes — 65
7. Opportunities (flow chart) — 79
8. Advertisement sheet — 83
9. Curriculum Vitae — 88
10. Example application form — 92
11. Example person specification — 93

Preface

Children deserve the best, and this includes the people working with them. The work can be both extremely demanding and immensely rewarding. If you consider you have what it takes to balance these expectations then read on: the questions you may ask before committing yourself to this career plan, the experiences and training to allow you to progress, the variety and responsibility to give you satisfaction, are all described in these pages.

I began my career in an education nursery, moving over many years to work in health services, the voluntary sector, with Social Services, further education, and local authority. I have worked with children in sickness and in health, with disabilities and with none, in direct service and in management, in training, policy and research, in registration and advice, from conception to adulthood, from student to parent, and raised my own, and at no time can I say I have been bored. Working in the childcare field has also given me undreamed of opportunities – travel around the world visiting childcare establishments and children in their own families, collecting traditional toys and many friendships along the way. It has, however, not been the easy option. I have had to work hard over the years, continually training, re-training and keeping up to date with issues, being open minded, seizing opportunities, becoming involved in emerging areas, presenting a commitment which demands high standards and respects the professionalism of others.

My greatest contribution would be to encourage others to come into the profession, to help in maintaining the provision and to develop staff, and for many able people to gain the satisfaction I have from the work. The benefits would undoubtedly be for the child.

None of this could I have achieved alone. I have worked and do work with some highly professional people, who stimulate me to keep moving on in my career. Denise, Daksha, Loraine, Caroline,

Carole, and the rest, I thank them all. And I thank all of the people who responded so willingly to requests for details for this book. To Sue Griffin of the National Childminding Association, Dennis Hemingway of The Scottish Childcare and Education Council, Sue McDonough of Nursery World, the many unknown respondents who popped items in the post, answered my telephone enquiries, suggested other contacts, and acted so willingly. Thanks to Roger Ferneyhough who allowed me the opportunity to express myself in a style, and content, I felt comfortable with. And to my husband Alec who, in his usual quiet manner, supported me with humour – and many cups of coffee.

Children are our future, and for that I dedicate this book to my beautiful granddaughter Kate Victoria Thompson. She has a right to the best, maybe **you** will be one who cares for her or all the other little children with equal rights.

Meg Jones

Is This You?

School leaver   Parent

                     Childminder

Imaginative   Caring

                     Hardworking

Playgroup helper   Unemployed

                     Retired

Organised   Creative

                     Friendly

Dance teacher   Nurse

                     Redundant

Energetic   Sensitive

                     Sympathetic

Sports worker   College leaver

                     Diplomatic

Committed   Calm

                 Brownie/Cub leader

Foster parent   Returning to work

                 Playscheme volunteer

Grandparent   Nursery nurse

                       Flexible

Assertive   Approachable

1
Working with Young Children

PREVIEW

In this chapter we will look at:

- making decisions about working with children

- examining your own qualities

- assessing what skills you have to bring

- considering what arrangements you need to make for your own children

- looking at the financial considerations in your own circumstances.

CONSIDERING YOUR OPTIONS

Straight from school

Young people considering a career with children have a number of options: practical, professional and academic. Openings may exist as an untrained nursery assistant, although opportunities will be few, pay may be low, and prospects limited. To test your aptitude a better option might be youth training, where experience and basic training could lead to further opportunities. College based courses with a less academic content will offer preparation for future assistants, while demanding professional courses can lead to satisfactory career progression. Academic courses equivalent to A-Level are also available.

Part of family responsibility

For many an interest in childcare flows from an increasing involvement with their own children based around family commitments. This may be childminding at home, being drawn into the playgroup movement, or as a parent helper in a nursery. Being at home with the children is not an excuse for not starting on a satisfactory career when the opportunities arise, in both urban and rural locations.

Fed up with the job

For some the time comes when job satisfaction is more important than continuing to earn by a means which is boring, inconvenient, or in some other way unsatisfactory. Having identified working with children as the area for which the sacrifice is to be made you need to be absolutely sure you are making the right decision, and make the best use of your opportunities. You will probably start off by undertaking a qualification course to make it worth while, although this might be alongside paid work to support your financial needs.

Redundancy and after

We live in an insecure world and for many there is no choice in having a career break, it is forced upon us. The fortunate will use the experience positively to assess their skills and interests and go for the career they perhaps have always longed for. No one wants to be in a precarious situation a second time, so careful consideration of appropriate training and options is essential to ensure the strongest possible position.

Drawn into the community

It is not unusual to hear in reference to childcare that 'anyone can do it'. This is just not so – you must be prepared to learn your trade. Within the childcare field are many openings if you are alert to the opportunities. Individuals often become involved in childcare through a series of life events. Progressive involvement as your own children grow may offer opportunities through parent and toddler group organisations, childminding, as a playgroup management committee member and parent helper, an assistant in an out-of-school club, or volunteer helper in cub scouts or Girls Brigade. A whole spectrum of experiences is awaiting the enthusiastic, from the newborn, babies and toddlers, pre-school, early years at school to special interest groups and uniformed organisations.

Questions and Answers

I think I would like to work with children but I am not sure I have the right attributes and background. How can I find out if it is worth my while pursuing childcare as a career?

If you are not able to see the qualities in yourself ask your friends, they can probably see a lot more than you. You may well be pleasantly surprised, or even astounded, at the areas identified. It will give you a basis on which to build, and additional confidence. Listen to what others say, good or bad. Build on the positive, work on the negative. When you have more awareness and confidence in yourself, then is the time to make your decisions.

I have been involved in many activities as a volunteer, over the years, as my own children have been growing up. Now they are at school I want to follow it up as a career but I am not sure which aspect would suit me best. Who can tell me what is best?

Careers officers, staff at your local provision, childcare information services, local colleges and this book will all give different perspectives on the work. Only you can decide what you want to do and ultimately the most appropriate way of getting there. Begin by talking to people in the business, reading relevant publications, enrolling on appropriate level courses, and gaining as much information as possible. You may be pleasantly surprised at the professionalism of it all.

WEIGHING UP THE QUALITIES REQUIRED

In order to work with children under the age of eight, paid or unpaid, you will be expected under the Children Act 1989 to meet certain requirements. The legislation refers to this as 'fit person', meaning suitable, and Social Services is responsible for checking out details. They will be looking for caring attitudes, physical and mental health, some awareness of multi-cultural issues, relevant experience and training depending on what you will be doing, and confirmation that you have not abused children.

What have you been doing so far?
Make a list of all areas you consider yourself reasonably proficient in, not only the easily recognised skills obtained in previous employment or at school, but also life experiences. You may be a good cook, cool in times of crisis, organised, enjoy helping children to read, have patience, have practical skills, be creative, be good at making money stretch, or have a host of other experiences to list.

Identifying your strengths
From your list of personal attributes (see Figures 1 and 2) and skills you will be able to identify where your strengths lie. Be honest about where you are at, and build on your positive qualities. Having identified the strengths you will no doubt also be able to recognise the gaps, which you can start to fill in preparation for the work. You will be surprised at how much you can learn about yourself.

Giving yourself confidence
You may have surprised yourself by your list. The greatest sap to confidence is to tell yourself that everyone you meet is more experienced, has more knowledge and greater understanding than you do. This is unlikely to be true. We all have different experiences, contributions to offer and support to give. Remember everyone has to start somewhere and if you want to *you* can learn. The mistake is to compare yourself with someone who may have been doing the job for years. Think of yourself as that person in three or ten years' time and convince yourself that you can get there too.

Tick those attributes that apply to you.

Patient	_	Caring	_	Communication skills	_
Non-judgemental	_	Cultural awareness	_	Valuing diversity	_
Tolerant	_	Reassuring	_	Supportive	_
Warm	_	Equal concern	_	Flexible	_
Creative	_	Organised	_	Healthy	_
Stamina	_	Dramatic	_	Energetic	_
Enthusiastic	_	Committed	_	Hard working	_

Fig. 1. Listing your attributes.

Tick appropriate column	Agree	Disagree	Don't know	
1. I think my way of bringing children up is the only right way	❏	✓	❏	1
2. I enjoy being with children	✓	❏	❏	2
3. I could cope with changing nappies/wiping noses/wet pants	✓	❏	❏	2
4. I would like to learn more about children and childcare	✓	❏	❏	2
5. I am prepared to put myself out/attend training	✓	❏	❏	2
6. I can get on well with children and can talk to adults	✓	❏	❏	2
7. I know something of other cultures and want to know more	✓	❏	❏	2
8. I can read the same story seven times without becoming irritable	✓	❏	❏	2
9. I could not work with a child with a disability/because of race/in a dirty condition	❏	✓	❏	1
10. I want to help children to learn	✓	❏	❏	2

Scoring: Questions 1, 9 – Agree score 1, Disagree score 2.

Question 2, 3, 4, 5, 6, 7, 8, 10 – Agree 2, Disagree 1.

A 'Don't know' to any question has a non score.

18

The maximum score is 20 points and the nearer you are to that the more suited you are to working with children.

Fig. 2. Attribute self-assessment form.

TRANSFERRING YOUR SKILLS

What are your interests?
Many people underestimate the relevance of skills gained in one sphere to another. You may not have worked with children before but you will be highly skilled in a number of areas:

- Can you play a musical instrument or sing?

- Are you a cartoonist or dressmaker?

- Are you into aerobics, languages or cooking?

- Do you like working with numbers?

- Are you a good organiser, an effective communicator, a sensitive listener?

All of these attributes will be useful in your chosen career. Caring for children is a complex task – do not underestimate it. You may have been operating at a higher level and need to scale your expertise down to a simplified form for the children to access. There is a balance between the two. A child may occasionally enjoy a favourite piece of opera, but much of the time prefer a noisy participatory rendering of 'The Wheels on the Bus'. Your language skills may help settle a bewildered child or your knowledge of food hygiene ensure freedom from food poisoning when you make shortbread. The service as a whole could profit with you as treasurer, or staff benefit from a communication course.

Previous work experiences
Think about your previous work experiences and how you might adapt them. Even very young children are using computers, can you help? Dealing with customers will assist you with parents, particularly in difficult situations. Having knowledge of a subject area like geology or growing vegetables will enable you to pass on valid information and develop activities in a simplified form.

Practicalities from home
A wealth of useful activities takes place in the home. Gradually we acquire these skills without stopping to assess their worth.

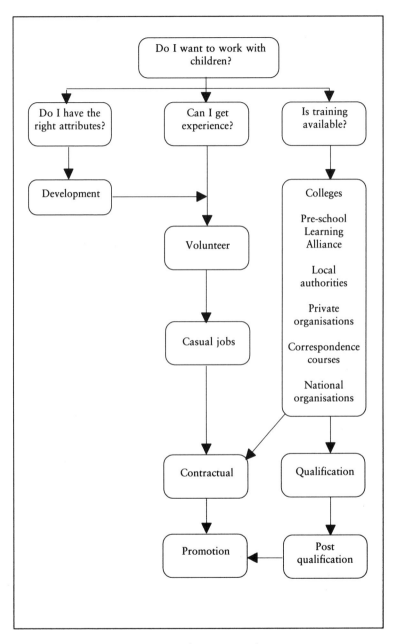

Fig. 3 Personal assessment form.

Working with children is a field where many come into their own: the cook, first aider, carer, gardener, comforter, story teller, cleaner, listener. Be prepared to adapt ideas from one age group to another, to simplify or extend.

Convincing others
Having assessed yourself now is the time to convince others of your worth. Being positive about yourself will take you a long way. If you do not sell yourself how can you expect others to buy? If you apply for a job knowing yourself, you are less likely to be taken by surprise. A confident person gives a better impression.

COPING WITH YOUR OWN CHILDREN

Taking your children
People assume, often wrongly, that a job with children gives you the automatic right to have your own children with you while you work. There are a number of reasons why this is not always possible: for example, a workplace nursery where, under equal opportunities, nursery officers should not be given preferential treatment over other employees but would be expected to wait their turn on the waiting list. Or your own children may be much younger than the age group you are working with and activities would be inappropriate for them. Or a free crèche in a sports centre, there to serve participants of an activity: if staff brought their own children along there might be few, if any, places for the public. Some parents are only prepared to consider jobs where they are able to take their children with them. This is possible, although it will limit the opportunities available. Childminding is the one option where you can guarantee fitting your own childcare around your work.

Will they want you there?
Another consideration is, while it might be convenient to take the children with you, will they be able to cope with sharing a parent with other children? Some children find this quite threatening and react by throwing temper tantrums, making excessive demands, clinging and showing signs of insecurity. It is very difficult to concentrate on the job in hand while all this is happening. There is also the status of the child to consider. Part of a child's growing

up, its independence, is to make a break from parents. Taking the child to work with you may hinder that development.

Do you need a break from them?
To be professional you need to treat a childcare job with the same approach you would expect of a solicitor or fire-fighter. You need to give it all your attention. The parent also has rights and for many it is important they are recognised as individuals with skills and attributes unrelated to their position as a mum or dad. The needs of the children and the wishes of the parent should be taken into consideration when decisions are made.

Fitting in with school hours

Restricting your opportunities
Anyone is entitled to impose whatever conditions they want on the sort of job they are prepared to accept. Childcare is no exception. But, as with any other job, the more restrictive you are the fewer the opportunities will be. Having said that childcare has, perhaps, more opportunities than most for you to choose to work within certain time constraints, and to bring your family with you.

Jobs in school hours
A number of areas of work operate within school hours. The obvious ones are within schools themselves: nursery class, teaching, parent and toddler group, community college crèche. Playgroups often, although not always, run term time only, road safety officers may have term time contracts, as will many trainers, and some childminders choose this option.

Jobs outside of school time
For some the best option is to work outside school hours, maybe because there is another parent or a carer available then to care for little ones. Others may wish to have a job where they can take their own children with them. Opportunities will be found in out-of-school clubs, activity groups, uniformed organisations, swimming lessons. In the school holidays there may be play-schemes, story telling sessions, full time careschemes.

Looking for childcare
You may need to make arrangements for your own children to be

cared for. The age of child/ren, type of job, family support, availability of provision are all factors which need to be addressed when seeking or accepting jobs. Childcare is not cheap. Justifying the expense requires an earning potential greater than the costs. Parents sharing care or close relatives are the most inexpensive choices, fitting work around provision – free place, nursery class – next, followed by childminders and day nurseries. Some parents are prepared to forgo income in order to gain experience, trusting eventually that a higher paid post will make their sacrifices worth while. Some work may be on a casual/standby basis only, consequently flexible childcare is also required. As well as family support some childminders may be prepared to offer short-notice flexible arrangements.

Weighing up the pros and cons
Besides making satisfactory work-time provision for their children parents also need to consider how to accommodate those occasions when they are ill. Being torn between commitments to children and obligations at work can make life very difficult. If you are unsure how you will cope with the dual demands perhaps it would be wise to try first as an volunteer on a regular basis, but where your absense would not be crucial to the running of the organisation. You will then be able to assess how easy or difficult it is for you to sort your childcare out, to get to work on time, and to accommodate the unexpected.

All year round provision
Consider the implications of taking a job running at times when children are not at school – even if you chose term-time work some holidays may not coincide, there may be teacher days off or schools closed for other reasons. Check if nurseries have compulsory closures for holidays and whether your choice of job can accommodate this. Inadequate preparation will cause difficulties and stress, contingencies will prove invaluable. Look for back up support.

CASE STUDY

Jo's career takes an unexpected turn
Thirty-five-year-old Jo was drawn into working with children

when she was asked to help out at her children's playgroup. The former financial assistant suddenly found she was enjoying the close contact with other people's children. She was encouraged to attend a basic playgroup course and went on to take the Diploma in Playgroup Practice. While on this course the opportunity came for her to apply for the vacant playgroup assistant post where she could regularly apply the skills she was learning. Her oldest child, Chloe, was by now at school but she could take four-year-old Jack with her. As the playgroup only operated during term time, school holidays presented no problems.

Once both children were at school Jo was able to change her job, and was offered a playgroup leader post one bus stop on from school. The job is not highly paid but has given Jo skills and experiences which have helped her cope with the demands of family life, have interested and motivated her, and which she has been able to work round her commitments. Now her children are older she has gained a mature student place on the BTEC nursery nursing course which she hopes will take her into working with disabled children eventually. 'I thought taking a break to have children was just a short term thing,' she smiled ruefully, 'but I find it has become immensely rewarding and now I don't want to do anything else.'

CONSIDERING THE FINANCIAL IMPLICATIONS

Childcare, as with any caring profession, is not renowned for paying high salaries. Indeed much childcare is very poorly paid, if at all. Other rewards, however, can be great.

Experience versus pay

There are few career opportunities in any field for the inexperienced. Fortunately in childcare it is possible to be welcomed as a novice, where you can gain the necessary experience, as long as you are prepared to accept little or no pay. The positive side is that you can move on, often in stages, from volunteer to a salaried position. Think of it as a short term sacrifice to (a) allow yourself to test out your suitability for the work and (b) to gain experience, and hopefully training, in order to move on. Children left in your care are a tremendous responsibility so experience does count: you have to prove to parents your competence.

Starting with a little

Start with what is local and easiest for you to manage, and accept that payment may be low or nil. Be prepared to accept casual or standby work as a means of gaining experience and getting your name known. Take advantage of any in-service training offered as volunteer or paid worker. If you have to pay yourself look for bargains: free or low cost courses may be offered by play organisations, local authorities, or community colleges. The more substantial courses can cost several hundred pounds a year so be prepared.

Affecting benefits

Receivers of benefits are advised to discuss earning position and any claimable expenses with your benefits officer. Easing into work on temporary, casual, or even volunteer basis is not made easy. I have known people to be affected immediately even when they would not receive any income for up to eight weeks, whose benefits are stopped for long periods on the basis of a few hours' work on an irregular basis, and others who could take their pay slip into the office and have it correctly adjusted on a monthly basis. Volunteers can be penalised if they offer too many hours. Once you know what the position is, it is easier to work within the constraints. Working for love, or expenses only, suits some people at certain points in their life. Opportunities for substantial experience, with high levels of responsibility, are available in playgroups, playschemes, organised groups, occasional crèches, and regular but short hours paid sessions as coaches or crèche workers.

What is the potential?

From low pay to career status
Payment for childcare varies enormously. It may range from £1 an hour on a casual basis, up to £20–30,000 per year for higher management responsible for managing provision. A qualified nursery nurse could expect perhaps £10,000 a year full time.

DISCUSSION POINTS

Working with children is a fulfilling and satisfying career.

1. Have you talked to your family or friends about your ambitions or about the issues around support and childcare?

2. How easy will it be for you to collect training information from centres accessible to you, and to talk to students and former students so you can make an informed decision?

3. What knock-on benefits of being involved in the community, such as contributing to your child's status, can you think of?

2
Gaining Experience

PREVIEW

In this chapter we will investigate:

- taking whatever opportunities for experience you can

- valuing volunteer or casual work

- using any special skills and interests you have

- using experiences positively in your personal development.

LOOKING FOR THE OPENINGS

Taking advantage of the opportunities

Initially some parents find themselves being drawn into activities their own children are involved in, before feeling they would like to commit themselves to working in the profession. Others see it as the opportunity they have been waiting for. Take advantage of the openings your children present by offering your services as an extra helper, utilising your skills, supporting activities. Search your neighbourhood for schools, groups or activities that you might be involved in. Your children might introduce you to the openings, or you could introduce your children to experiences they may otherwise not have found. There is likely to be a range of experiences available if you are open minded and willing to try different age groups. There is a whole range of opportunities in all age groups around the country, but you may have to travel out of your immediate locality to find some of them. Here are some examples:

Doing voluntary work
Be alert to opportunities so keep an eye on local papers, radio appeals, adverts in shops, or word of mouth that volunteers are required to work with children. You can expect to have to complete forms and give permission for checks to be made on you to clear you as a 'fit person' under the Children Act 1989. If you have regular free time and no contacts get in touch with your local Volunteer Bureau and offer your services. There you will be interviewed to identify your interests and link you up to the most appropriate organisation looking for volunteers.

Joining a parent and toddler group
For many their first excursion into group childcare is through a parent and toddler group, or Bal Mandir, the Asian versian. Those first tentative steps into the world of mothers and babies, (and some rare groups of fathers and infants) will give you an idea of the demands of large numbers of little children vying for attention, the level of activities required, and how to satisfy the dual needs of children and parents. As you become established in the group offer your services – as coffee maker, book keeper, activity helper, play organiser. Use the experience positively. A well organised parent and toddler group offers a range of opportunities, and frequently because of the nature of the group there may be little opposition if you choose to take the lead. The experiences can lead on to other things. Bring to the work experience skills gained in other places, make them work for you in the new situation, and add to them.

CASE STUDY

Paul finds his niche
Paul's interests were in music and politics. Unemployed and in his early 20s he accompanied his friends to political meetings, often held in the homes of people mostly his own age, some with young children. Paul was drawn into amusing the little ones while their parents were in heated debate. He enjoyed the experience. A community organisation offered government training schemes for mature candidates in childcare and Paul successfully gained a place.

After the one year placement he knew this was the career for him. A spell as a paid casual worker led to a permanent post of crêche assistant and on into NNEB training, where as one of the few males in the profession he was particularly welcomed. On completion he gained further experience in day nursery. He was able to fit in his interest in music both inside and outside the job, gaining uncritical acclaim from the children for his guitar playing. The training and experience eventually took him to work in an education nursery, which allowed him time to do the job he loved and indulge his passion for composing in the school holidays.

'My political friends taught me about the inequalities in society and the disadvantages many people experience,' he said. 'Having a caring male as a role model is a new experience for many children, and it can do nothing but good. What's more it's good for me too!'

Taking casual work
Do not ignore the opportunities casual work can offer: there are some valid and varied experiences to be gained. Casual work might be appropriate for the less experienced, but also for the qualified looking for a way back into the profession. There may be facilities near you where the opportunity to gain experience on a paid casual basis may be available. Contact your nearest sports centre, local council, community college – or any organisation likely to be offering childcare alongside activities – to see if they employ casual staff. For the older children playscheme staff may be employed on a casual basis. The occasional casual job can lead on to regular sessional work or permanent contracts. Do not dismiss casual work as being limited or limiting as much valuable experience at all levels can be gained this way. Being paid to gain experience is not to be dismissed.

LOOKING FOR ESTABLISHED GROUPS

There are many areas where experience can be gained in a voluntary or paid capacity. Some are explored below.

Volunteering in a playgroup

Parent helper
The playgroup movement was founded on the premise that parents would be actively involved in their children's development through play. Parents are therefore very welcome and positively encouraged

Nursery nurse		Playgroup leader
	Au pair	
Parent and toddler group		Teacher
	Playworker	
Nanny		Special needs worker
	Bal Mandir	
Nursery teacher		Crêche worker
	Opportunity group	
Playscheme worker		Carescheme worker
	Toy library	
Childminder		Children's nurse
	Maternity nurse	
Red Cross		Rainbows
	Beaver Scouts	
Story teller		Children's librarian
	Themed groups	
Sunday school		Activity groups
	Leisure activities	
Sports workers		Resort childcare
	Universal Aunt	
Residential childcare		Foster parent
	Shoppers crêche	
Family centre		Private nursery
	Montessori nursery	
Dancing class		Commercial activity groups
	Uniformed organisations	
Hospital play therapist		Childcare manager
	Nursery officer	
Nursery assistant		Workplace nursery
	Playbus	
Inclusive play		Assessment centres
	Lunch-time supervisor	

Fig. 4. The variety of work with children.

to become helpers. Many playgroups have a rota so parents know when they are expected. They are likely to be counted in the adult/child ratios, thereby being of vital importance, and have clearly defined tasks to do. Do not be alarmed if you are inexperienced – you will not be asked to do more than you are capable of. It will probably mean sitting at a table supervising an activity, making the mid morning drinks, or accompanying the other adults with the children on a walk. However, it is important to the smooth running of the group that you attend on the days and times you are expected.

Valued assistant
It is not unusual for regular parent helpers to be invited to be assistants when vacancies occur. This may be a paid or unpaid post. Even when paid, remuneration is likely to be small. Payment, however, is not a determinant of the range of experience you will have, compensations are in confidence building and having something to offer others.

Becoming a leader
With the experience gained, along with appropriate training, the next logical move is to become a playgroup leader. Again, depending on the type of group and circumstances, leaders may be paid or unpaid. The responsibilities will obviously be greater so, in addition to the variety of activities provided, the leader will gain organisational skills and team building experience from working with the parents and co-ordinating of the day-to-day operation.

Opportunities in an Opportunity Group
Opportunity Group is the term applied to a pre-school group catering for disabled children and their non-disabled siblings. Other similar groups may be known by different names. The group will offer the sort of play activities you would expect in any playgroup or crêche, with some additional resources, adapted equipment and extra adults. If you have experience of disability, in your children, family, or personally, or a particular interest, you may wish to offer your services to one of the groups. Often a number of professionals will be involved – health visitors, paediatric occupational therapists, speech therapists, teachers *etc* – and this experience will give you a greater insight into the work as well as providing a valuable service to the community.

Using the terminology

Having a disabled child is often a traumatic, if positive, experience for many parents. Not only do you have to be caring but you must also recognise the parent's expertise with their child, and adopt a sensitive approach in dealing with the parents. It is advisable to be familiar with the terminology used before working in the group: the parents have enough to contend with without you making insensitive and inappropriate remarks. What was acceptable ten years ago may not be today.

Acceptable words	Unacceptable words
Disabled	Handicapped
Learning difficulty/disability	Mentally retarded
Wheelchair user	Wheelchair bound
Cerebral palsy	Spastic
Limited mobility	Cripple
Downs	Mongol

Fig. 5. Acceptable/unacceptable words

Helping out at school

Memories of your own schooldays will influence how comfortable you are, or not, with current schools. There is a perception among some that schools are unapproachable, parents should stay at the gate, only entering by invitation or if things are going wrong. Teachers have been trying to dispel this myth and actively encouraging parents, grandparents and community members to come into the school. Areas to be involved in include listening to children reading, craft activities, bi-lingual work, fund-raising activities, one-to-one work, accompanying children on school trips and to swimming lessons. Talk to the class teacher and find out what help they need; if you have particular skills offer them to the school. We all have more to offer than we give ourselves credit for. As you become more familiar with the set up and gain confidence you will find more opportunities, more often and more regularly, opening up. Gaining experience in a school will enable you to assess the job opportunities, see if it's the sort of work you would like, and so prepare yourself for application when posts are advertised. You may be interested in ancillary work, one-to-one support for a disabled child, nursery nursing, teaching, lunch-time supervisor, library assistant or crossing patroller.

Preparation for Home Start
Home Start is a voluntary organisation supporting parents with pre-school children who, for whatever reason, are experiencing difficulties. Volunteers, with support from the organisation, visit families, befriending, listening, encouraging. The only condition imposed on volunteers is that they should be parents themselves.

To move from being 'just a parent' into a volunteer with status is a very important step for many. It can mean the transformation from being Paul's wife, or Sheena's mother, into being a person in your own right. You have standing and value within your community. In order to know how best to support families, what confidences must be kept, what resources are available, how to think through issues, and how to get to know organisers and associate volunteers, a course of preparation is offered. This is valuable training and that, along with experience of working with families and in Home Start groups, is useful preparation for a long term career in working with children.

Questions and Answers
I'm new to the area and would like to work with children. I previously helped out at my daughter's playgroup, but she is at school now, and I don't know where to find local provision. How can I find out where groups are?

There are several possibilities to try. Social Services are required by law to keep a register of all provision for under eight-year-olds running for more than two hours a day. This may be inspected in person, or a list may be supplied by your local authority. The local branch of the Pre-school Learning Alliance will have a list of all member playgroups; and childcare information services in some cities, community services councils in rural areas, and libraries may have such information.

I have had a lot of experience as a volunteer over the years but never got around to any training. Will this prevent me from getting a paid job with young children?

It will not automatically exclude you from all jobs, but it will significantly restrict your earning powers. The Children Act 1989 requires that staff not only should have relevant experience but that at least half should be qualified. Without training you could be an assistant, but will probably never progress to being in a position of responsibility. If you would be satisfied with a low pay, low status job then go ahead. However, by taking one of the many training/qualification routes you could increase both satisfaction and income. A range of qualifications is acceptable: see Chapter 6 for further details.

Action points
To make as many opportunities as possible to get into paid work, or gain a training place, keep your options wide.

- Spread your experiences over a number of settings.

- Use the skills you have.

- Attend any training available.

- Keep up to date with issues.

- Learn from others.

USING YOUR SPECIAL INTERESTS

Playing for the nursery
If your skills and interest lie with music, and particularly if you play an instrument, you will be more than welcome in the nursery. Many teachers and nursery staff rely on singing and tapes for their musical accompaniment and having the volunteer services of a musician, even a basic one, can liven up the day and add new dimensions to the routine. If you can set up a regular session, dance, music and movement, mini aerobics, musical stories, and other activities can be programmed into the children's day. Although centred around a specific activity, this is valuable

experience in working with young children, particularly if you are an active participant in the group. In addition you can learn through observing nursery staff, what they do, and how they interact with the children.

Sharing your culture

Celebrating festivals
Do not underestimate the particular information you have, your way of life, the religion you follow, the festivals you celebrate, the food you eat; they could all be of interest to others not sharing those experiences. Schools, nurseries and playgroups welcome input from members of the community willing to give information, be involved in cultural activities, bring in artifacts, tell stories. Celebrating festivals in the group is a community cultural event, not a religious conversion exercise, and as such adds interest and aids children's understanding of others.

Cooking with the children
A commonly shared experience, particularly for special events, is cooking and eating. Is this an area where you could share with young children? Fortunately children accept many things relatively uncritically, and with humour, so there is no need to be shy if you do not possess masterchef skills. Keep it simple, quick, and with visually attractive results and you will invariably impress the children. Children have an avid appetite for new experiences so even just bringing ingredients in will extend their vocabulary, develop their senses, and break down some of the myths of difference – a valuable experience for both you and the children.

Sharing your lifestyle
You may well have some interest or lifestyle experience which may be unfamiliar to the staff working with the children, which the children can either relate to or learn about. Offer your services. Areas you might consider include:

- language skills
- dance and/or music
- photographs and mementoes of other lands
- clothes to dress up in
- hair plaiting/beads or flowers

- food and cooking
- print making/crafts
- Rakhi/friendship bracelets.

Serving in a Sunday School
Many churches have a crêche during Sunday services and can offer opportunities to work with babies and toddlers in groups. Because the time spent in the crêche is usually very short it is unlikely to be registered under the Children Act, but should still be run according to the spirit of the law. This gives, perhaps to the relatively inexperienced, the opportunity to find out acceptable conditions, provide suitable toys and equipment, and practise organising a small group of very young children. The experience can be very valuable. During family services stories may be told, music participation encouraged, drama performances arranged, little children kept amused. There may be opportunities to organise some of these activities and be involved in programming.

Take this opening to find out about resources available for this age group and read up and learn as much as you can. Help in Sunday School. During school holidays many churches have playschemes based on a Christian theme. The age group is likely to be 4–8 or 5–10 years and will involve games, crafts, story telling, team work, organisation and planning.

Supporting the sporty
If you feel your strengths lie in health, fitness, or sports activities you could be made welcome within sports clubs, uniformed organisations or activity groups. Volunteers help leaders and coaches to supervise children as they develop their skills, safe from accident and harm. Many a start in working with children has come about through volunteering to help at the local gymnastic or swimming club. A lively interest will start you off, leading to training as an assistant, and ultimately gaining coaching qualifications if you choose to develop these strengths. Often sports groups and classes are built on the personality and enthusiasm of the coach. To progress it is essential to have appropriate awarding body qualifications.

Personal development
For a time it may be fulfilling to be a volunteer, to be involved in local initiatives, but for most the time comes when you are ready

to move on. Initially this may be into nominally low paid work like playgroup, or maybe into casual play or crêche work, eventually leading to permanent employment. Do not be complacent, keep assessing yourself and your personal circumstances and be ready when the opportunity arises. To use the experiences you have gained you should take the opportunity to undertake training, read about the subject, attend conferences, share ideas, keep up to date about initiatives and current thinking, in order to move on.

DISCUSSION POINTS

1. What would be the pros and cons of volunteer work for you: contributing to society, gaining confidence and skills, gaining experience, job satisfaction, minimal income . . . ?

2. Which local agencies might be able to help you find the opening you need?

3. Responsible jobs are sometimes offered on a casual basis: could there be any near you?

3
Working with Babies and the Under Fives

PREVIEW

In this chapter we will discuss:

- working in groups
- working in the home
- working in the health field
- special needs children
- specialist groups.

UNDERTAKING GROUP CARE

Managing a day nursery

Local authority provision
Most local authorities provide day care, particularly for children at risk of being removed from the family home. This is not to say it is exclusively for disadvantaged youngsters as some authorities operate a mixed economy with free places, employee bought-in places, and fee paying. While open full time many free places are only part-time. It is more usual for children to be aged between one and five years, with some baby places. The staff need to be well trained, experienced, to set the standards, and have a thorough awareness of social issues – particularly around child protection. A typical career path would be to start as a qualified nursery officer, to become senior nursery officer, deputy manager and manager.

Workplace nurseries
Supported by businesses, organisations, and authorities, workplace nurseries provide childcare for employees, often at a subsidised rate. The benefit to the employer is retention of staff who are costly to recruit and train and who, without such a facility, may not return following maternity leave. They offer full day care provision, the opening hours responding to the needs of the organisation as far as possible. Parent user groups may have more influence over policy than in some private nurseries, because employers listen to what they have to say, and if it would benefit a large number of their staff they are more likely to change conditions. Fees may be more flexible than in the private sector as employers can choose to help lower paid workers. Some workplace nurseries may be contracted out to organisations specialising in childcare.

Private sector
Run as businesses private nurseries mostly cater for working parents, although some may be education nurseries. Because of the nature of the provision many nurseries will take babies from a few weeks until school age, and increasingly are taking children up to eight after school. As with all full day provision minimum standards and registration under the Children Act 1989 apply. Unlike local authority or workplace nurseries private nurseries receive no subsidy, therefore sufficient income must be gained from the parents to cover costs, and inevitably, as with all businesses, outgoings will be kept as low as possible. This may mean that fewer qualified staff will be employed, although still within the regulation minimum of half, and wages may be low. It does give opportunities for unqualified staff to gain employment.

Working in a children's and family centre

Professional work with parents
Managed by Social Services a range of different services is offered in family centres to, as the name implies, support families with young children. There may be the traditional day nursery services, drop in for parents and children, play activity groups or a crêche while parents have speakers and activities in another room, training in parenting skills, child behaviour management groups, integrated provision for disabled children, respite care, disability

units. Qualifications for staff will vary from authority to authority; the centre may be run by nursery nurses or managed by social workers.

Social work aspects
Many of the activities in a family centre will be to support parents and children, and most will be there through social work intervention. Participatory work will be undertaken with carers on progress plans, focus on tasks or behaviour, risk assessment, and rehabilitation of the child into the home. Staff will need to develop relationships with the clients, carefully observing and recording behaviour, effecting change, weaning off dependency. Special skills and attributes are necessary for this work. Child protection work is a feature of Social Services nurseries with supervision, monitoring, case conferences, and evidence giving.

Leading a crèche
If you are considering work in a crèche you need to know which definition is being used. To some crèche means full day care, particularly a workplace nursery, and for others it's sessional care including babies. In the context of this book crèche refers to sessional or occasional care from a few months to a few years. This work may be permanent or casual. Crèches may operate on a regular basis with the same children attending each session, others may have irregular attenders on a first come first served basis, while some may be for specific events, conferences, training, festivals. It is demanding work requiring high skill levels, depending on the purpose and location of the crèche.

Valuable experiences
It can be excellent experience in taking responsibility, managing resources, supervising staff, organising provision, dealing with parents. Crèches may well be operating autonomously within a leisure or community centre and have little contact with the rest of the organisation, making the leader self-reliant and in control of this valuable provision. You will need to be clear about your aims and objectives, policies and procedures, the organisation's expectations and your own position. As the crèche may only be peripheral to activities going on in the centre this clarity is important for you to convince others of your worth in competing for valuable funding and gaining recognition.

OPTING FOR FAMILY CARE

Nannying
There is a great tradition of nannies in this country. The rich and titled have always had them, now a new generation of working parents are eagerly seeking out competent individuals who can give care and companionship to their children. Not all nannies are qualified, although many newly trained childcarers gain jobs with families. Pay rates and conditions will vary according to levels of experience and qualifications. A newly qualified live-in nanny could expect an average of £125 a week in London, and about £100 elsewhere in the country. A daily nanny can expect a bit more, £160 in London and £140 in the rest of the country. Averages always include higher and lower figures, of course, and unqualified nannies must expect people to pay at the lower end of the scale unless they can claim substantial experience. Conditions and contracts need to be clearly defined to prevent dissatisfaction and exploitation, one of the more common causes of complaint. Clarify whether you are expected to baby-sit, do general housework, cook for the family. Nannies could expect to have care of their charges, keep their toys, room, and clothes clean, and prepare children's meals; anything else comes in the realm of mother's help or *au pair*.

Sharing families
To suit parents' needs and finances sometimes they decide to share a nanny. This could mean spending half the week in one home with one set of children, and the other in another with different children. Alternatively it may mean children from two or more families are cared for in one of the homes. Providing there are not more than four children from three families, nannies have exemption from registration under the Children Act 1989.

Childminding
Childminders are by definition individuals who care for children under the age of eight in their own home, for more than two hours a day, for reward. The law requires them to be registered – this includes inspection of the premises and clearance as a 'fit person' of both the applicant and anyone else living in the home who will have substantial contact with the children. Childminding happens all over the United Kingdom in inner city, suburb, village, and

isolated country location. Generally childminders are self-employed and operate according to market forces; they are more likely to have a good take up if there is employment in the area and a shortage of childcare places. A few childminders will be employed, retained or subsidised by Social Services to provide places for children with special need, or at risk, for whom home care is the most suitable type of provision.

While fitting in around family life, childminders can offer more flexible care which suits many parents. Also as the children get older they can remain with the childminder, attending before and after school, if it suits minder and parent. Where groups of childminders can get together support groups are formed, training may be presented, and issues discussed. Childminders do a professional job in their own home.

CASE STUDY

Nadine is approved by Social Services

Nadine had worked in a toy shop before leaving to have her two boys. She had always enjoyed having children around her, having harboured a secret ambition to be a play therapist in her younger days. Now at home, not wanting anyone else to care for her own sons, yet with time and love to spare, she felt she could offer help to other parents who needed to work. The money would come in very handy too.

Nadine applied to Social Services and a visit to her home was arranged by a Registration Officer, who talked through the issues, inspected the property, and left a number of forms to fill in. Both Nadine and her husband David had to be cleared as they would both have substantial contact with any minded children. Personal statements were made, references taken up, GPs contacted, police and Social Services records checked. There was much checking to do to ensure Nadine's suitability, and the house was safe and appropriate. 'There was very little I had to do,' Nadine confided, 'because I have plenty of toys and fireguards and things. It took several weeks to get all the details sorted but I really enjoyed the pre-registration training.'

Since registration Nadine has minded Sarah, a four-year-old, during school hours and Jodie aged 18 months on Mondays and Fridays. 'This gives me plenty of time for the boys and a new outlook on life. David says he's never known me so satisfied.'

Partnership in playgroup

The playgroup movement can provide useful career opportunities. Although many playgroups are sessional and run on a shoestring, paying workers nominal sums, a few will be run by organisations and local authorities where hourly rates paid are comparable with nursery officer salaries. Recent developments have included extended day playgroups to cater for working parents. Many playgroups are members of the Pre-school Learning Alliance, the national organisation supporting and promoting playgroups. Opportunities arise within the organisation to develop and share skills gained in the practical setting with others with similar interests. This may be on local or national committees, as a field worker, in a resource centre, or as a trainer.

Questions and answers

I've always been surrounded by children, younger brothers and sisters and cousins, so I've plenty of experience. Is it really necessary to do training, as I would really rather be earning money?

There are some jobs you can get with the experience you describe and without training – mother's help, untrained nursery assistant, *au pair*, playgroup assistant – but you will find pay low and prospects limited. You will likely be competing for jobs with people who have more to offer than you, such as qualifications and experience in organised groups, which could leave you frustrated and unemployed. The best option would be to find a place where you can gain experience while gaining a qualification, like NVQ Level Two (see Chapter 6), although this will not be easy.

If you are really serious about working with children you will need to put yourself out, perhaps you could work in the day and take a childcare course in the evening. If you are looking for work locally try local newspapers, and national magazines like *Nursery World* and *The Lady* carry advertisements for family based jobs, often with accommodation.

Having gained my nursery nursing qualification I would like to work with hearing impaired children. What opportunities are open to me?

Try your local education department for details of specialised nurseries, schools, units, or mainstream schools with hearing impaired pupils, and specialist support services. Some authorities employ specialist nursery nurses (hearing impairment) to work on a peripatetic basis travelling to nurseries, schools, and making home visits as appropriate in their area. On the health side, with additional training, there may be audiology jobs in hospital departments. Other areas, while not exclusively with hearing impaired children, include private nurseries, day nurseries, health visitor's assistant, and Portage home visiting scheme. Alternatively you may wish to go on to do further training and could take a BEd degree and on into teaching hearing impaired children.

FOCUSING ON SPECIALIST CARE

Considering hospital work and health care

Hospitals offer various employment opportunities with children; however, many of them are of a specialist nature requiring specialised or additional training.

Play therapy
Most large hospitals will employ play staff to work on wards, in playrooms, outpatients and casualty departments. Their job is to encourage children to play as normally as possible for their age and stage, to promote play tasks which strengthen a child's malfunctioning body, to distract from the distress of illness, to ensure development is not delayed more than necessary, and to make what can be a negative experience positive. Play is a great stress reliever, it can help a child understand illness and treatment, builds confidence, aids diagnosis, and involves the parents.

Generally qualified nursery nurses, or children's nurses, undertake a further one year qualification course as a hospital play specialist for this work. Payment is set by the various NHS Hospital Trusts so will vary from place to place. The scales recommended by the National Association of Hospital Play Staff starts at just under £10,000 per year on a basic scale, up to a maximum of nearly £18,000 for a play co-ordinator on a managerial grade.

Maternity and baby care
Most opportunities with new mothers and babies will require nursing training. Midwives usually are Registered General Nurses who have completed a further 18 months' midwifery training, although if you decide from the beginning that is what you want to do you can take a three year pre-registration course. Special baby care staff are mostly midwives who have undertaken an additional six months' training. A few hospitals employ nursery nurses, who work with newborn babies, feeding, bathing, changing, encouraging breast feeding, and generally supporting mothers within the first days. A few opportunities exist for trained staff as maternity nurses in private homes to care in the first month or so after birth, particularly if there are special concerns over the new mother.

Specialisms in hospital
Staff trained in childcare may work in various departments of a hospital, paediatric assessment centres, outpatients, playrooms, specialist play workers, *eg* with child liver transplant patients. Qualified social workers may specialise in hospital paediatric work. It is not unusual for individuals with a childcare background to want to take their knowledge and experience of the healthy child, after further training, into work with the sick child. Children's nursing, a specialised form of nursing devoted to children, can be undertaken in just over a year following qualification as a Registered General Nurse (RGN), or as a three year pre-registration course. Likewise a qualified certified physiotherapist can specialise in paediatrics, as can occupational therapists.

Hospital schools
Hospital schools tend to be small, catering for a wide age range, in scattered locations – some in classrooms, others on various wards, and with many pupils only there for a short time. Pregnant teenagers with additional health needs may also receive education. This mix of constraints presents its own peculiarities. Staff will be trained teachers who have specialised in this area.

Caring for special needs children

Seeking out the provision
Opportunities to work with children with disabilities and special needs include specialised playgroups, Opportunity Groups, education nursery provision, special units in day nurseries, voluntary/charitable nursery provision, exclusive playschemes for children with physical disabilities or learning difficulties. Each region has its own range of provision and it may need seeking out. Places to find such information are Social Services, education department, British Red Cross, Volunteer Bureau, umbrella groups for voluntary organisations, specific organisations for disabled children – for example, Scope – local libraries, and childcare information services. As adult/child ratios need to be high, volunteers and extra workers are always needed.

Some people, who may not have had experience with disabled children, initially feel apprehensive or the weight of responsibility towards the children. Be reassured that this is quickly dispelled: as soon as the children are seen as individuals their disabilities take second place. Developmental steps may be smaller, but each minute achievement is experienced as a giant leap. The advantages of identified provision for children with 'special needs' are higher staffing ratios, ancillary care, appropriate physical environment, ease of access to multi-professional support, being with children with similar needs, reduced parental isolation, and proficiency of medical surveillance and administration of drugs where necessary.

Integrated provision
To work with disabled children it is not always necessary to seek out specialist provision: many children are accommodated in regular provision. There are advantages to integrated provision: parents may prefer it, children will be with their peers, can attend locally, and follow normal patterns of playgroup, nursery, reception class and primary schooling. Additional or experienced staff may be recruited to work in these areas to offer support and ensure the child gains full benefit from the experience.

GOING IN TO SELECTIVE CARE

Working in a Montessori group

Named after Dr Maria Montessori, the provision now mostly described as 'Montessori' has a particular philosophy based on a number of concepts. These are based on the child's natural ability to learn, providing the right environment, and being prepared for the appropriate time in the young child's life when they are ready to gain most from the experience. There is a structure to the learning, the development of self-discipline, a simplicity in approach. Children are encouraged to co-operate rather than compete, and gain awareness of the world around them. Montessori provision can cover age range nought to twelve years, although it is most usual in this country for two to six-year-olds. A Montessori training can prepare individuals to work in infant/toddler groups and nurseries, as nannies, and in primary schools.

DISCUSSION POINTS

1. Considering all the options, which age group or area most appeals to you? (Focus on that area when applying for jobs, that way your enthusiasm is likely to shine through.)

2. Would you consider areas outside your experience (you may find there are opportunities which give you great satisfaction)?

3. If your options are limited due to your own childcare needs, have you explored all the opportunities that exist both within the home and in the community?

4
Working with Older Children

PREVIEW

In this chapter we will explore:

- widening your range from under five to over

- considering if you want to work with older children

- looking at work in or outside school hours

- the crossover from playwork into teaching

- extending your working opportunities by different age groups at different times.

RUNNING A PLAY SESSION

Out-of-school club
A burgeoning area in many parts of the country, out-of-school clubs operate on school premises, in community rooms, neighbourhood centres and other accommodation. Supported through local industries, community grants, government funding, fund-raising and parental contributions, staff are appointed to run groups on a regular basis. Children may attend from the local school, or they may come from a large catchment area, in which case the club staff may pick them up. For two to three hours, until working parents can pick their children up, the staff aim to offer a relaxed environment where children can wind down after a day's education, play with their friends, have tea, activities and fun. Play is a professional job requiring knowledge of legislation, safety,

curriculum, dealing with groups, managing staff. There will be a playwork qualified leader or teacher, and assistants.

Leisure activities
Sports and leisure centres increasingly offer a variety of activities, providing work opportunities for the sporty active individual. These may be traditional sports activities such as teaching swimming, trampoline coaching or gymnastic training, or they may be associated more readily with other community facilities as in craft sessions and fun filled playschemes. Non-sports activity staff may be playworkers. Particularly for seasonal work, seek out opportunities in theme parks, zoos, community farms or recreation in parks.

Specialist groups
Activity groups targeted at certain sectors of the community may be provided: girls' groups, Asian dance, music groups, embroidery clubs, arts activities, pottery, printing, video sessions, cultural or language groups. These will require workers who have specialist knowledge, understanding or awareness – maybe developing out of playwork.

Co-ordinating a carescheme
A carescheme is a full time care project for school age children during the holidays. It is open for a full working day, similar to nurseries catering for working parents, with a probable age range of 5–8, 5–12, or 8–12 years. It differs from playschemes in a number of ways:

- the length of the day: nine or ten hours

- the care element: it cannot be open access, children must be delivered and collected by their parents

- meal times must be catered for: packed lunch or food provided

- the children may not be there by choice; working parents want their children to be there

- it will need to be registered under the Children Act 1989 as full day provision, as it is open more than four hours a day

- staffing ratios are likely to be higher, to cope with the demands of the long day

- it must be well planned and organised – to prevent accidents, occupy the children, and offer several weeks of **fun**. It is, after all, the children's holiday.

Providing for employees
Some careschemes will be part of an employer's package of family friendly policies. It will be supported, and maybe subsidised, by the employer. Some provision will be a direct service delivered by the organisation, others will have 'bought in' places to offer employees. Contracts will vary according to who is employing the carescheme staff. The work gives scope for developing skills and management opportunities, enables a wide range of activities to be tried and tested, is valuable experience, raises awareness in another field of work, and is tiring! Because the staff may not work together at other times there is need for team building, planning, and training, before the first child is admitted.

While it is not desirable to plan the fine detail without the children's input, a broad outline of activities, at least for the first week, is appropriate. The day needs to be structured, some activities booked, materials collected and bought. Staff need to be familiar with administration, policies, procedures, work instruction, Quality Assurance, criteria, back up, premises, equipment, roles and responsibilities. A shift system is likely to cover the length of the day, and because the scheme will be operating during traditional holiday periods carescheme staff will be expected to take off peak holidays themselves.

For students in training, or staff working term time contracts, this type of employment will give additional scope. Some careschemes may be extensions of out-of-school clubs, employing the regular staff with supplementary workers. A carescheme will need a co-ordinator and administrator, who will not be counted in the adult/child ratios, and a number of assistants on a ratio of one to eight.

On the open market
Not all careschemes are run by employers for employees, some are community groups or managed and operated by parents themselves. These may be supported by fund-raising, grants, parental

contributions, sponsors, willing local organisations, schools and colleges. The principles, however, will be the same as employee careschemes, although there may be need to actually set up all the systems, open bank accounts and, depending whether it's a 'one off' or first time, it may be a matter of learning on the job. A lot of expertise is available in the community and amongst parents – use it. Private nurseries are increasingly opening up their intake to 5–8 year olds after school and in the holidays. For this they will need suitably trained and experienced staff. A good carescheme team will cover a range of skills, experiences, background and training – playwork, sports coaching, teaching, nursery nursing, social work; and staff who include energetic, mature, artistic, ethnic minority and disabled men and women.

CASE STUDY

Priti's experience pays off

Priti had drifted into playwork, first as a volunteer on an adventure playground in her teenage years, later as a paid sessional worker, and then a play co-ordinator. As she had been gathering experience she had undertaken whatever play training had come her way: practical workshops, first aid, food hygiene, policy making, equal opportunities, a playwork foundation course. When she felt fully committed that this was what she wanted to do, she took the Playwork Certificate course. Along the way Priti had gathered a formidable amount of knowledge and experience. 'It was a surprise to me when I came to fill in the application form for deputy co-ordinator of the Carescheme a few years ago. I knew then that I was ready for this more intense care experience for a few weeks. Everything I had done before was useful, but I still had a lot to learn. Fortunately I worked for the first year with a very experienced leader, and she was a good role model.'

Priti noted what worked and what was less popular, how to plan a long day so that staff and children came out smiling at the end. She had never worked with such a large staff team and found the induction week extremely valuable in learning how to motivate a new group from a cold start into a fully functioning unit after five days. In fact some of the bonds were so strong they held tight at the end of the summer. 'I was invited to the wedding of two of the workers from that first summer,' she remembers.

The following year the previous co-ordinator moved on and Priti's chance came to put her own ideas into practice. 'It's a tremendous responsibility,' she said seriously. 'There are so many things to be aware of: Children Act, procedures, ensuring all the children are booked in and out, making sure there are sufficient staff if we arrange mini trips, being aware of food allergies – particularly nuts – and the things children get up to. You also have to watch other things the children bring in like adult videos, or gambling with pogs. Keeping the children occupied and safe from 8.30 to 5.30 every day for seven weeks takes some doing, it's longer than a school day. However, I was well prepared for the challenge, and it really was taxing, but it was good to feel I had succeeded, managed the whole thing, with only the odd little upset. The thing I remember most were the water fights, and always to take a spare set of clothes with me.'

Organising a playscheme

As the name implies play is the focus of this extended session run during the school holidays. Playschemes may operate for two hours, before a lunch break and a further two hours, although they will vary according to local needs. There is a wide variation in how playschemes are operated; they may be within the statutory sector, voluntary or community groups. Skills and experience play a vital part in presenting quality provision; in addition to playwork training short courses on playschemes are offered in some places. Some playschemes are run entirely by voluntary efforts, others are grant aided by local authorities. All over the country, in town, city, and village, playschemes will operate – often on a shoe string – with community support.

Assisting in a primary school

Schools may employ classroom assistants either on a permanent or temporary basis. To cope with the fluctuations in school rolls ancillary staff may be employed on short term contracts. As teachers' assistants the duties could include preparing materials, supervising groups of children, toilet visits, helping to ensure the smooth running of the day. Specific posts may be created to support a child with special needs on a one-to-one basis. Staff may be qualified nursery nurses recruited specifically for that job, or drawn from a list of supply staff held on a local authority list, or unqualified with the right attributes. Working in the middle of a school day suits some lifestyles, and lunch time supervisor could be a solution. Over recent years the profile has been raised as more professionalism has been brought into the job, including training, with some areas encouraging a resurgence of traditional playground games. Although not strictly a school job, but fitting around school hours and employed by the local authority, is the job of crossing patrol man or woman.

Questions and answers

We have all been children once, some of us not that long ago: isn't play just something we do? Why do we need to train to be a playworker?

Playwork is a demanding job requiring a range of skills and those gained as a participant are very valuable. However, in taking part you are only responsible for yourself, following the rules, and being fair to others; as a playworker you are responsible for organising others to ensure equity, safety and lawfulness. This requires knowledge and experience from a different perspective. You need to know about legislation, about getting the best out of people, equal opportunities and managing diversity, to have an overview of the curriculum, how to manage difficult behaviour, planning and organisation. In training you will learn how to balance the formal aspects with the informal, the serious with the fun. As with any other job the more you learn the more you find there is to learn. Do not underestimate the professionalism of it all, if it looks easy it's probably because someone has worked hard at it.

I have an NNEB qualification, having worked in a primary school for the past four years. I am now ready to try something different, probably working abroad before I get tied down with family commitments. I'd like somewhere with a bit of life in it. Any suggestions?

There are opportunities to work with children in a number of European holiday destinations, if you fancy the sun and sea as well as energetic childcare activity. A number of well known companies employ qualified staff to run clubs for the children of holidaymakers, either on campsites or attached to hotels. Experience can be gained with children from a few months to twelve years or more. Look for a reputable company offering good backup, training, high staff ratios with qualifications, and management support.

Some companies offer nurseries for different age groups, under one year, toddlers, 3–6 years, 6–12s, and the staff are expected to organise play and activities, expeditions and beach games. You may be expected to do baby rounds or babysit in the evening, and as the service will be available seven days a week you must be prepared for an intensive experience.

If you have sufficient experience there may be the chance to manage a number of staff, or a group of children's clubs and nurseries. Off duty you will have access to the beach and watersports. The work will be seasonal, probably from April to October, but valued staff may have the opportunity to spend the winter season working in a ski resort.

HOLIDAYING WITH PAY

Working the ski slopes

Generally referred to as 'nannies', childcare staff are recruited to work in chalet crêches, and as snow nannies with the older children. You must, however, be prepared to turn your hand to domestic duties as well as looking after the children. Experienced childcarers may be offered senior posts with responsibility for a group of workers. You will be recruited in this country, for the season, and will need to demonstrate how you would keep children of different age groups occupied and happy every day of the week, while their parents are out on the slopes.

Except in exceptional circumstances nannies must be prepared to work the whole of the contract, and you will not be disadvantaged because you cannot ski. Payment is not high, but board and lodging are offered so you do not have to worry about that, and there are compensations if you are interested in the sport: on days off you will have free ski hire and free ski passes. You will have to be very resourceful and deal with lots of different children, experience which will support applications for work back in the UK, or for returning for another winter season on the slopes. This is a very competitive field as hundreds of hopefuls apply for the relatively small number of jobs; as with any other you need to be well prepared, motivated, and committed.

Camps in America

Every summer sees a huge exodus of young people leaving Britain to work in summer camps in America. Job descriptions require enthusiasm and fitness, energy and resourcefulness, someone who will not themselves get homesick and who can comfort others who do. In addition to liking children particular skills are also welcome: sports, arts, music, cooking. Called **councillors**, recruits could be placed anywhere in the hundreds of sites across America, where the fortunate children are able to spend time away from parents – sleeping under the stars (or not sleeping at all), rafting and water-sports and all those things 'mom' would be afraid for them to do, cooking communally, and generally having an action-packed few weeks. The fare, accommodation, and a small amount of pocket money are paid, and you will have the opportunity to travel for a week or two after your contract to see a bit of America.

Activity holidays in the UK
Opportunities exist to work on summer camps, activity holidays, in holiday centres, and with organisations offering play and sports for disabled or disadvantaged children in various centres in the UK. The age range is five to 15 years, so there will be plenty of opportunities to extend your range of experience. Some posts will be childcare, some sports coaching. Generally accommodation is provided, possibly travel with the children to the camp site, and pocket money from £30.00 onwards. Qualifications will depend on the post applied for: some will only require enthusiasm and experience.

Care in the Kibbutz
A steady stream of the young (and not so young), students, and newly qualified head every year for a few weeks' or months' work on an Israeli Kibbutz. While specific jobs are not guaranteed, where people have special skills particular experiences will be offered if possible. However, you must be prepared to try all sorts of different occupational tasks. Employment in a children's house, or *gan*, could be valuable experience for childcarers. The opportunity to observe childcare in a different culture gives insights into the diversity evident in the UK, of which we are not always as aware as we might be. An English speaker immersed in a non-English speaking environment will have a greater understanding of the experiences of young children in an alien environment where words are incomprehensible, giving rise to confusion and distress. Different cultures also have different expectations and it is useful

to consider levels of dependence/independence, language development, potty training, extended family/multiple carers, educational standards, and to bring those experiences and understanding into other work situations.

TEACHING

Early years

There is an increasing expectation that four-year-olds should have definable 'learning outcomes' from forms of pre-school provision, as preparation for school and life. These are nothing new, and many pre-school providers have been producing the results for years. The range of activities expected cover physical development; awareness of space and movement; mathematics, pattern and counting; creative development through texture, colour and sound; language and literacy with books, expression and writing their name; knowing the world around them by exploring the environment and living things; families and events; and personal and social development through sensitivity to others, working in a group and learning independence. All good provision will offer these outcomes. Early years teachers are trained to work with 3 to 8-year-olds in an education setting: nursery classes, four plus units, reception classes and primary schools.

Combined centres

An attempt to redress the divisions between the different types of provision, a combined nursery centre offers full day care and nursery education in one location. Staffed with both nursery nurses and nursery teachers, the centre has an extended day, with a nursery operating during traditional school hours and caring provision offered either side of this and integrated into the day as appropriate. Working conditions and contracts for the different staff vary and this can cause some conflict, serving to demonstrate the difficulties in overcoming the fragmentation of under five services. Combined centres may also offer out of school provision.

DISCUSSION POINTS

1. If you want to work with older children, are you prepared for high energy activities and higher noise levels?

2. Have you thought about working for a short time in another country, assuming you have no ties?

3. Do you know of local examples of the different types of provision mentioned here?

5
Searching for Other Initiatives

PREVIEW

In this chapter we will cover:

- considering your own business venture

- the appeal of changing the environment

- the family fit approach

- enjoying the variety of childcare in all its glory

- ideas for activities.

SETTING UP A SHOPPERS' CRÈCHE

Coping with young children while trying to shop is a nightmare for some parents, so a shoppers' crèche is a popular option for many. Set up by local authorities, shopping complexes and arcades, and voluntary groups, the provision offered and the job opportunities will be varied. The crèche may only be open for two hours once a week, or full time six days a week. It will need to be registered under the Children Act 1989, so staffing ratios and conditions will be dictated by this. Half the staff will need appropriate qualifications. Ages of children will be varied but it is likely to be 18 months up to eight years. Shoppers' crèches need to be particularly well organised, because most of the children will be strangers to one another, and maybe to the staff, and there may be a wide age range. Activities and the environment must be immediately attractive to persuade the child to stay, and the staff must be experienced in community provision.

Problems particular to a shoppers' crèche relate to the contactability of the parents in case of distress, incident or accident. Safeguards need to be built into the system like settling children in, only allowing the youngest ones in for a maximum of an hour for the first few visits, asking parents to telephone in to check their child is OK, insisting children are collected on time, having emergency contacts in case parents are unable to return (think of accidents or sudden illness), and ensuring the child is returned to the right parent.

PROMOTING CHILD FRIENDLY CITIES

Making the environment safe and welcoming to children and their parents is an increasing concern that will take us into the next century. Businesses, local authorities, voluntary organisations, Chambers of Commerce and trade associations are looking at joining forces to promote child friendly facilities in their locality. Some have formalised the arrangements to establish 'Child Friendly City' status, assessing shops, restaurants, health facilities, and public services and giving awards as recognition of good practice. This developing service offers job opportunities to individuals with childcare backgrounds and interests who also have skills in marketing, presentation and administration.

Questions and Answers

I have an idea for setting up a small business offering childcare to a conference centre near my home. What do you think? Where do I go from here?

Have you discussed your proposals with the conference centre? Assuming they are interested you need to find out what is needed to register with Social Services. Work out a business plan to ensure your ideas are viable, taking into account staffing, equipment, administration, depreciation, insurance and profit. Staff appointed to run the service will need to be appropriately trained and experienced, and you would need to be certain you had enough competent workers to provide the care. You will need sufficient toys and equipment to offer a standard of service acceptable to the conference centre. Your commitment would be to provide a service when required, so draw up a contract to ensure both parties are clear about responsibilities and commitments, and good luck.

I have worked in the public sector and found it rather bureaucratic. I think I would like to work in the voluntary sector where I will not feel lost in the crowd. What sort of jobs might be available?

A whole range of childcare jobs is available in the voluntary sector, from very small groups, substantial local centres and regional trusts, to very large national organisations. Remember all organisations will have certain restrictions – legal constraints, organisational procedures, financial regulations – and all will be accountable to someone. Funding agencies will require that certain criteria are met, as will the Charity Commissioners. Consider the options carefully, you may well find some organisations are just as bureaucratic as your earlier experiences, whereas others will be less so. Think of the variety:

- a community run playgroup, managed by a committee of parents, with membership of the Pre-school Learning Alliance, for which you may have a free hand to develop your own policies and practices

- a crêche in a Women's Centre where you will be a specialist worker. You will need to assess how much control you will have over your area of service delivery. Establish if policies are set by crêche workers, centre manager, management committee, or by local authority funding agencies

- a nursery supporting disadvantaged and distressed parents, part of a national network, with directives being passed down from an executive board

- a special needs resource centre, part of a national organisation, but allowed to develop its own services appropriate to meet the needs of the community

- a 'one off' converted bus offering a toy library service to parents and children in isolated rural locations, where a small core of employees work with a select support group to run the venture.

KEEPING FIT

Coaching children
There are junior sports clubs, classes and activities for practically every sport available to adults. Some of the more popular ones are gymnastics, football, swimming, mini rugby, martial arts, trampolining, judo. For every one there is a sporting body setting the standards. Generally sports staff work with adults and children, although some specialise with younger customers. While involvement with children often evolves, specialist training is available to work with this age group.

Caring in leisure facilities
Over the past ten years a revolution has taken place in private and public sports clubs, leisure centres, fitness centres, gyms and neighbourhood centres offering physical activities. Care for users' children has become important politically, economically, and in equalising opportunities. Crêches to support activities are now a regular feature. Some are sessional, targeted alongside certain activities, others full time to accommodate a range of opportunities being offered in the facility. Some will take the same group of children week after week, others will be drop in. The advantage of on-site provision is that if a child does not settle, is very distressed, or has an accident, parents can be recalled.

The crêche will need to be registered if it is running for more than two hours a day, at least half the staff will need to be appropriately qualified and experienced, and the staffing ratios will be high if babies are admitted. Rates of pay will vary, but should be comparable with other forms of childcare in the locality.

CASE STUDY

Sue returns to work
Having her own children raised all sorts of unexpected issues for Sue when she felt they were old enough for her to consider returning to work. 'I needed something I could fit in around my own childcare needs and something I had confidence in doing. This last thought was a surprise to me,' she confided. 'It's amazing how being out of the field for a few years makes you feel so out of

touch.' She giggled at this point, because before having babies she had been a deputy manager in a day nursery, and everything she did revolved around little ones. 'I mean I was sure caring for children hadn't changed, but the expectations of staff had, policies, Children Act, and even the words used – like curriculum, we used to say activities, and child protection instead of child abuse, new descriptions like small world play, and anti-discriminatory play. I had taken short courses when I could, and been involved in my own children's play opportunities, but I still felt a bit nervous.'

When she saw an advert for a crêche leader in a leisure centre she thought 'here's a piece of cake,' she'd just do it for a few months to get her confidence back and then move on into other things. 'I was wrong,' she admitted. The job proved to be much more demanding and stimulating than she had imagined. The interview had been pretty tough to start with, it was a good job Sue had kept up to date with current thinking; but she did get the job and found herself in charge of three assistants and up to 20 children, five mornings a week. 'I found my previous training and experience were put to good use. Because the children were there for only two hours, there were often new ones in, parents had little time to settle them in because they were off to play sport or attend an aerobics class, we found working together as a team and planning for the session extra important.'

There was only half an hour to set up before the session started, and half an hour at the end to clear away, so discussion and planning had to be fitted in there. With limited equipment the staff have to keep setting the room up in different ways, be inventive in the use of materials, use resources available to them like unfashionable saris for dressing up or draping over chairs as a tent. 'I've been doing it now for three years, thoroughly enjoy the in-service training we get, and can get the satisfaction out of seeing a job well done while parents get that much needed break. I can't see me moving on just yet.'

However, if Sue does eventually change jobs she will have a lot more to offer a new employer: experience with a wide age range – six months to five years all together – constantly dealing with new children, managing staff, using limited resources wisely, being responsible for the admin, the day to day planning and duties, training inexperienced assistants, ensuring equal opportunities are met, dealing with leisure centre staff. She has also gained up to date knowledge and understanding, references, and confidence in her abilities, as well as widening her remit. And 'the money has come in very useful too,' she grinned.

ORGANISING CHILDCARE AT SPECIAL EVENTS

Local authorities, voluntary groups like the Pre-school Learning Alliance, and interested individuals and groups may offer childcare and associated facilities at local events. Some will be paid work, some voluntary. Garden parties, city and county shows, cultural events, festivals, music promotions, trade shows, business exhibitions, promotions in shopping centres, conferences, and fun days can all make demands.

Facilitating local initiatives

Mobile crèche facilities may be required (see below), but also other types of provision:

- Play areas where staff set up, supervise, and pack away, but where parents remain responsible for their children. These could be targeted at particular age groups, or offering restricted activities – painting and crafts, obstacle course, cooking.

- Nappy changing and feeding facilities.

- Story telling.

- Face painting.

- Parent and children rooms used as withdrawal areas from the main, often busy and noisy adult activities, set up as a crèche but parents are expected to stay. These may well operate late into the evening when regular provision would not be appropriate.

- Running children's parties.

- Erecting and supervising inflatables.

- Organising non-competitive games.

- Painting competitions.

- Thematic activities.

- Lost children facilities.

- Supervised softplay.

Mobilising childcare

Childcare can be presented in many forms and a growing area, under a variety of names, is mobile crêches. This is where play and care are offered, in places where crêches are not normally held, to support parents who are attending conferences, training sessions, festivals, open days and events. They may be managed by local authorities, voluntary organisations, or be in the private sector. If there are fewer than six in a year then they have exemption from registration under the Children Act. This type of provision should not be taken on lightly; it requires thorough and knowledgeable planning. The event needs to be booked well in advance so that premises are identified, checked out for safety and suitability, equipment appropriate for the space selected, sufficient staff recruited, and Social Services informed.

If the provision is offered more than six times in a year on one site it will require registration under the Children Act. If there is regular childcare in the premises at other times and you can share facilities and equipment this makes it much easier. If, however, you have to import everything then you will need to arrange transport, check you have enough materials to last the day, a wide enough range of equipment to suit all ages, stages and abilities, have appropriate registration documents for details of the children, daily register, conditions of use, maybe cleaning materials, possibly a mobile phone if no other is available and parents are in scattered locations, *eg* on a university campus. You need to be clear about your responsibilities and commitments.

Questions for clarification
- Do you get a lunch break?

- Are the parents coming into the crêche to feed the children at lunch-time?

- Are you expected to feed the children?

- What ages are you catering for?

- Are places pre-booked?

- What will you do if you are full and two more children turn up?

- How much will you be paid to run the service?

- Who should you communicate with on the day if there are problems?

Creating a themed session
A popular proposal is for a mobile crêche running alongside a conference, activity or event to have a theme in keeping with the adult content. So an adult music festival could have a musical crêche, or a Greenpeace conference an environmental theme. Although not often suggested by the organisation booking the crêche they are usually delighted if a themed session is proposed.

A good group of childcare workers, in a brainstorming exercise, could come up with a range of appropriate activities, equipment, stories and outcomes around a given subject if encouraged. Basic equipment and materials could be adapted to fit the theme: sand, water, recycled materials, painting and crafts, dressing up, adaptations to the home corner, layout of the room, selective use of jigsaws, books, stories and rhymes. The staff could be given names, *eg* Red theme – Julie brick, or brick Julie, Sheela bright, maroon Fiona, Adam pillarbox, Jyoti scarlet. Without a subject associated with the adult activity organisers are often pleased to be offered something a bit different, like a focus on creative play, natural play, or at an outdoor event in a park a physical activity.

Figure 6 shows the start of a plan around the subject of environmental play. You can build up a range of regular, developed, or occasional activities around a central theme.

Other themes which could be developed in a similar way include:

- Music.

- Sunshine trail – a physical activity circuit marked on the ground in the shape of a sun (or any other design). Along its path could be tunnels, beams to balance on, a crash mat with

Fig. 6. Ideas springing from the theme of environmental play.

a painted sun on, climbing through a sun-shaped hole cut in yellow painted cardboard box, climbing frame, crawling under pegged down saris. The list goes on.

- Messy play – sticking, painting, waterplay, papier-mâché, hand and foot printing, cooking, cocofibre on sheet on the floor, cornflour and water, jelly in water, stories about 'mess'.

- Multi-cultural.

- Food.

- Colours – deck all the activities out in particular colours – say green and blue – select plastic and wooden toys predominantly in those colours, books about colours, football team displays in those colours, blue table cloths with green plates in the imaginative café, green and blue playdough, shades of green and blue paint and paper, make green vegetable soup, staff dress in green and blue.

- Gardening.

- The world.

- Ourselves.

- Science – shop with scales and loose goods, waterplay with sinkers and floaters, colour mixing, ice cubes in water, cooking, sand with wheels, funnels, and varied containers, hospital corner, paper making, study plants and make displays.

- Maths.

Playbuses
Converted buses, single or double decker, old or new have been a cheerful, if expensive, alternative play provider since the seventies. For staff and supporters playbuses bring a range of emotions from euphoria at seeing the brightly painted object trundling around dull estates or bland landscapes, to despair at the cost of another tow-in. Staff experience fulfilment of servicing the needs of parents and children in a flexible, exciting, interesting manner, and the misery of a cold snap and trying to coax an unwieldy machine to warm up, spark, and get going. It's not the place to work if you are claustrophobic, mind being overheated in the summer or frozen in the winter, or have a bad back as there is a lot of lifting and moving things around. But for the right personality and commitment the compensations outweigh the disadvantages and it can be great fun.

The type of provision offered on a playbus will vary according to funding briefs, management committee directives, parent organisation's wishes, or terms of reference, as appropriate. The nature of the playbus can mean being in different places on different days of the week. It may be a playgroup, play session, parent and toddler group or ·crèche perhaps on one deck while parents are being counselled, attending a group, or learning English on another. The playbus may serve as a toy library, or resource centre. Many will be adapted to accommodate disabled children. Some will offer specialist facilities, for instance the National Deaf Children's Societies 'Listening Bus' is fitted out with technical equipment and aids, including minicoms, with advisers on board to support parents and children. Staff will need skills relevant to the activities offered. In addition to childcare and parenting experience you will also need to be fit, and may need to drive.

DISCUSSION POINTS

1. Do you agree that, because working with children is labour-intensive, to cover costs high prices must be paid by users unless subsidies are in place?

2. If you are thinking of providing mobile facilities, can you store equipment for 'between times'?

3. Expectations of users will be high and you will need to be on top form all the time. Does this appeal to you?

6
Training and Qualifying

PREVIEW

In this chapter we will look at:

- making the right decisions in the first place
- choosing the most appropriate course
- 'it's not only what you do, it's how you do it'
- alternative ways of getting there
- portfolio building.

SEEKING ADVICE

The Children Act 1989 is clear in its guidance and regulations that for full day care 'at least half the staff should be qualified in childcare, early years education or social work' and in sessional registration 'in all cases at least half of the staff should hold a relevant qualification in day care, or education, or have completed a training course specified by the Pre-school Playgroups Association (now Pre-school Learning Alliance) or other voluntary body' and that other staff should be encouraged to follow relevant training courses. Great emphasis is placed on individuals to take relevant courses and gain appropriate qualifications, particularly if they wish to develop their skills and move on into management/leadership roles.

In working with people who have undertaken childcare training it is not uncommon to come across individuals who have been badly advised on which course most suited their aspirations. There are so many courses available it is difficult for the uninitiated to distinguish one from another. It is too large an investment, in time, money, and commitment, to take lightly. Do not rush into training. Courses, and the way they are presented, are being continually reviewed, extended and changed, so find out about as many as you can. Seek advice from as many sources as possible: colleges, careers offices, employers, awarding bodies, articles and books, registration officers, and most specifically from people who have taken training and where it has taken them. Look in the Useful Addresses section to gain further information.

CHOOSING A COURSE

The various courses, although with the same ultimate certificate, will differ in presentation and opportunities dependent on the individual colleges, tutors' expertise, local placements, days or hours of commitment at college, and mix of students. So if you have a choice of college consider these elements carefully – they could make the difference between you getting the most out of the course or not.

CACHE

A modular one year Certificate in Child Care and Education (CCE) is validated by the Council for Awards in Children's Care and Education (CACHE). Providing the underpinning knowledge for NVQ Level 2, there are 14 modules assessed by assignment, multiple choice question papers and practical skills. This certificate will prepare you for work as an assistant; it can, however, be used as an entry into the second year of the NNEB Diploma.

NNEB

The National Nursery Examination Board Diploma is a leading course, recognised nationally, for the childcare professional working with the birth to eight age range. It can be taken over two years full time, or on a modular basis, or part time over a longer period in England, Northern Ireland and Wales. Check out with local colleges for the most suitable option for your needs. If you take this course be prepared to work hard, give up your social life, and have a satisfying and fulfilling experience. The course combines practical experience and theoretical training through placements in different settings, with all age groups, and attendance at college.

There is continuous assessment of the 21 modules in both college and practical work.

NNEB module titles

1. Observation and Assessment
2. Work with Young Children
3. Induction
4. Equal Opportunities
5. Foundations to Caring
6. Physical Care and Development
7. Social and Emotional Development
8. Health Care 1 (including First Aid)
9. Learning through Play
10. Cognitive and Language Development
11. Children's Behaviour
12. Food and Nutrition
13. Work with Babies, 0–1 year
14. Health Care 2
15. Child Protection
16. The Nursery Nurse in Employment
17. Child Care and Education in Britain
18. Disabled Children and their Families
19. Working with Parents
20. Social and Legal Framework
21. Early Years Curriculum

Scottish Child Care and Education Board

The Board is the professional awarding body of Scotland with certificates at two levels: Preliminary Registration and Registration. Courses are presented in colleges and through Scottish Vocational Qualification (SVQ) accredited centres. Colleges offer a one year programme of the Scottish Vocational Education Council (SCOTVEC) National Certificate modules which leads to Preliminary Registration with the Board. This can be followed by a separate one year programme leading to a SCOTVEC Higher National Certificate in Child Care and Education and to Registration with the Board. A range of modules developed around the National Occupational Standards is offered, individual colleges identifying those appropriate to their locality plus units specifically required by the Board. Make enquiries at your local colleges or contact the address at the end of this book. SVQs at levels 2 and 3, and other qualifications or combinations, will also be considered for registration at an appropriate level.

BTEC courses

Relevant courses validated by BTEC include National Certificate and Diploma in Childhood Studies (Nursery Nursing) and Higher National Certificate and Diploma in Early Childhood Studies. The National courses can be taken full or part-time over two or three years, have an entry requirement of four GCSEs at grade C or above, or BTEC Intermediate GNVQ, or equivalent. Core subjects covered are human growth and development, practices in childcare, early childhood learning, child health, legal aspects and social policy, and professional practice. In addition, depending on the college and interests of student, a range of options is undertaken. Work placements of 800 hours in nurseries, hospitals and voluntary organisations are part of the course. The BTEC Childhood Studies (Nursery Nursing) qualification is given as a relevant qualification under the Children Act 1989, and considered along with NVQ level 3 and NNEB. BTEC National in Childhood Studies meet general entry requirements for related degree courses, Higher National, and training in nursing, social work and teaching.

Higher National qualification in Early Childhood Studies prepares students for managerial roles in the early years environment. It also provides for enhanced access into degree courses. Entry requirements are BTEC National, A-Level and GCSE, Advanced GNVQ, or equivalent. Compulsory subjects include professional studies, interpersonal and communication skills, learning and development, and social policy and legislation. Optional subjects cover pedagogy, curriculum – language – mathematics – science, early years information technology, and managing people.

Pre-school learning courses

The Pre-school Learning Alliance offer a number of courses ranging from one day workshops, informal 'doorstep' courses, short basic courses, to a diploma; taking place locally in further education and community colleges, schools, village halls, nurseries and pre-schools. At whatever point you are coming into childcare work there will be a PLA course to suit your needs.

The most substantial of these is the Diploma in Pre-school Practice which is recognised as a qualification under the Children Act, particularly for playgroups. The course involves the study of theories of how young children develop and learn, and its application in pre-school work. Curriculum, record keeping, parental involvement, management, equal opportunities, and the underpinning knowledge required to take an NVQ in Childcare and Education are addressed in the course. It is also possible to take the diploma through distance learning. Other short courses are aimed at specific areas: play, parent and toddler, child development, curriculum, administration, under twos, under fives first aid, special needs, and equal opportunities. Experienced staff may take a tutor/fieldworker course.

Montessori courses

The Montessori method recognises three elements as being essential to this particular approach:

1. Universal characteristics of childhood – each an individual, creative potential
2. The prepared environment – harmonious surroundings, freedom to work and move
3. The special qualities of the teacher.

A range of training is offered through from parents' courses to BEd (Hons) degrees. Diplomas can be gained in different age groups – birth to three years, three to six years, birth to six years, six to nine or six to twelve years, preparing students to work with children in various capacities. By taking a series of courses it is possible to move from a Diploma to a degree, or NNEB to Teaching Diploma. Entry requirements will vary according to the course ranging from one GCSE to eight, two A-Levels to post-graduate. Most courses have examinations, practical experience may be compulsory or encouraged – depending on the course or validating body, and integral or additional workshops are available lasting between one and ten days.

Different accreditation is given by particular Montessori training centres and you will need to be certain you are gaining the most appropriate qualification for your circumstances. Montessori training is recognised the world over, and many overseas students come specifically to the UK to gain the qualification; this adds cultural dimensions to the student group not obtained in other types of training.

Courses may be accredited by the Association Montessori Internationale (AMI), the International Montessori Accreditation of Teachers and Schools (IMATS), and the Open and Distance Learning Quality Council (ODLQC). For future employment it is important to consider that Montessori establishments have particular requirements and specify Montessori training as an essential for staff.

Childminding

The National Childminding Association has developed a model of training courses ranging from preparation courses for new childminders, follow-on training for the first year of minding, to in-service workshops for the experienced. The Association produces training materials to give tutors around the country the tools to deliver the courses. The material provides the underpinning knowledge for the NVQ in Childcare and Education. Opportunities vary depending on where you live and childminders would do well to put pressure on local authorities to provide relevant training.

Playwork training

Two part-time courses piloted through experienced playwork trainers are presented through the National Kids Club Network. For newcomers the 64-hour Playwork Foundation course gives a framework to the issues, practical advice, and underpinning knowledge required of an assistant playworker. The course has been linked to the NVQ standards in Playwork at level 2. Experienced playleaders, working as part of a team, can take an 84-hour higher level course, Investing in Playwork, which covers the areas outlined in the NVQ standards at level 3. These courses are run nationwide, by approved trainers, and receive funding from local Training and Enterprise Councils. Distance/flexible Learning Programmes are being piloted by the Kids Club Network to meet needs of workers in rural areas.

A range of specialist training programmes and workshops is also available. For a more advanced course several colleges and universities around the country offer a two year full-time Diploma of Higher Education in Playwork.

Hospital playwork

Hospital play specialists are professionally qualified with an NNEB, Cert Ed, Registered Sick Children's Nurse, or equivalent, who undertake an additional one year college course to gain the registration of HPSET (Hospital Play Staff Education Trust), validated by BTEC. The course is presented at a number of colleges around the UK, and in Hong Kong, although many fewer than offer standard childcare courses. Inevitably places are limited and competition fierce. No places are offered to students under the age of 20 as the nature of the work requires maturity to deal with the stress of working with disturbed and seriously ill children, with all its implications.

The course consists of block training, block placement, plus one day a week at college for one year. Subjects covered are child development, play as a therapy, awareness of basic nursing routine and medical techniques, and practical sessions on adapting play for the sick child. Visits to hospitals and relevant places are made. The Hospital Play Specialist qualification is gained by continuous assessment both practically and academically, timed assessments, and a project selected by the student.

Bi-lingual childcare courses

In communities with high levels of ethnic minority populations courses of preparation to work in childcare may be offered in heritage languages. These courses give the candidates confidence to communicate, recognise the skills they already have and can develop, enabling them to get into the job market, paid or voluntary. Some colleges in Wales are able to offer bi-lingual courses up to and including NNEB in the Welsh language.

Questions and Answers

I like the idea of NVQ, because I would find it difficult to attend a college course and I have gained a lot of experience over the years. Is it the easy option?

Definitely not. For the qualification to be meaningful you have to demonstrate to an assessor that you have knowledge, understanding, and practical experience to the required standard. In order to do this you have to collect evidence, answer questions, and be observed at work. It requires effort on your part; you will have to learn what you need to know, what needs to be recorded and collected, and how to organise this information. It will be hard work, nothing of worth comes without effort, but if you want qualifications, have sufficient knowledge, and find working largely on your own resources suits you then go for it. The sense of achievement at the end will be worth it.

I know I want to work with children, but I am not sure yet in which capacity. It might be nursery nursing or teaching. How can I avoid making a time wasting mistake?

By taking the BTEC Diploma in nursery nursing. You will be able to do this between the age of 16 and 18 as an alternative to A-Levels, at the end of which you will be qualified to practise as a nursery nurse. Should you then wish to move into teaching, many universities will accept this as credits for entry to an Early Years degree course, or Bachelor of Education (BEd) degree. By taking this course you will be giving yourself breathing space, gaining a nationally recognised qualification, and preparing yourself for an academic course at some time in the future.

ADCE

Experienced nursery nurses are able to enrol for the modular Advanced Diploma in Childcare and Education, full time over one year, part time over two to five years, or through distance learning. Six modules are taken, one of which is an elective chosen for a dissertation, the individual colleges choosing from a selection validated by CACHE, the Council for Awards in Children's Care and Education. Students need to be working with children, in health, education or day care setting as course work is linked to practice. ADCE enables students to gain professional knowledge, skills and practice, raises awareness of contemporary issues and new developments, and enhances career and professional development.

ATTENDING TRAINING

Many of the factors referred to in Chapter 1 relating to work with young children need to be considered with regard to training: commitment, cost, childcare arrangements and support of family. It is not the easy option. In reality some courses are more difficult to accommodate than the work to follow, because if you decide on one particular course you will not be able to pick and choose attendance – flexibility is likely to be limited. However, if you prepare yourself, arrange satisfactory childcare for your children, tell yourself 'you can and you will' complete the course, then you will do it. Many colleges and organisations are aware of the limitations of busy people juggling home and family, jobs and training, and the trend is towards modular, part-time, flexible, evening and distance learning, where possible. It may be that one place offers one pattern while somewhere close by offers another. Look around and choose the one that most suits your needs. Many colleges also provide childcare while you study.

CASE STUDY

Sian overcomes her deafness to win a college place

Sian thought she would never be able to achieve her dream to work with children. As a teenager friends and acquaintances told her she would not be offered qualification training, which she knew she needed, and even if she did no one would offer her a job. Although profoundly deaf, she had attended mainstream schooling and had done well in her GCSEs. No one, however, had taken account of her determination. 'I knew what I wanted to do and I wasn't going to accept no for an answer.' Knowing the competition for places was acute Sian was anxious to gain experience to demonstrate her competence and commitment before applying to colleges. 'I was unable to get paid work,' she confessed. 'For a start I was unqualified and secondly people were wary of my impairment.' In the end she volunteered to work in a local playgroup and, after an initial cautiousness, was readily accepted for her bubbly personality, attitude and awareness rather than her limitations.

Much to her surprise three colleges offered places, two on CACHE certificate and one for BTEC Diploma. 'The tutors were really understanding,' she said, 'much more than I expected. They all took time to explain things, and no one objected to my bringing my sister with me to help if I had difficulty interpreting any words.' In the end Sian accepted a place at the college she felt most comfortable in. 'This one is so used to having disabled students it's no big deal. They have all the facilities, support staff, flashing light fire alarms as well as bells, induction loop throughout the building, even sub-titled videos. It's great.' Having been successful in her first year Sian went on to the NNEB Diploma course. 'I'm not expecting it to be easy to get a job,' she says, 'but I do expect to be able to compete equally with other newly qualified people. Having got this far has given me the confidence to achieve. Nothing will stop me now!'

ASSESSING THE ALTERNATIVES

Correspondence courses

Following courses by post could suit the needs of some people. Consider the value of the outcome in relation to your career expectations before committing yourself, as they will not all be readily recognised in the market place. Some courses will require you to follow a standard course (PLA Diploma, ADCE, for example) with instruction to gain experience in certain practices/activities with children in a location convenient to you. These will be recognised by employers on a par with usual methods of gaining training. Others will provide knowledge without expectation of practical experience. A theoretical course without practical experience will gain you limited work in childcare when you will be competing against others who have followed more traditional routes.

The NVQ/SVQ route

National Vocational Qualifications and Scottish Vocational Qualifications are nationally recognised qualifications aimed at people already in work. Rather than attending a knowledge based course and coming out with a qualification, NVQ/SVQ candidates are assessed in the workplace where their competences to undertake the job are recognised. Of course candidates have to have knowledge appropriate to the level being assessed, but this can have been gained from a variety of sources:

- any courses attended over a period of time

- private reading: books, magazines, documents, research papers

- attending conferences, seminars and workshops

- TV programmes and videos

- personal projects and study.

NVQ/SVQs are being developed in the areas relevant to working with children and can be gained at various levels. Based on standards of good practice level two is appropriate to assistant responsibilities, level three to supervisor/leader, and level four to development. Candidates register with an Assessment Centre and are assigned an assessor, who may be one of your colleagues from your workplace or from elsewhere. At each level what are called performance criteria are described which the candidate must be able to demonstrate competence in. This is assessed by the assessor through observing the candidate at work, through questioning, inspection of evidence collected in a portfolio, log books and diaries, assignments, photographs, action plans. The assessor will advise you, but the progress is candidate-led and therefore up to you to make sure it is completed. You will need to be highly motivated to complete the qualification and it will be easier if you have contact with other candidates to support one another.

Childcare and education
The NVQ/SVQ qualification will prepare you to work with the younger end of the age group, including babies. Level 3 in Childcare and Education is considered equivalent to NNEB.

Playwork
Largely concerned with five plus age group, NVQ/SVQ will give you relevant qualifications to assistant, run, and manage play provision.

Coaching children
If your interests are on the sports side coaching NVQ/SVQs include units pertinent to working with children.

Building a portfolio
A portfolio is a valuable collection of documentation which will demonstrate to assessors or prospective employers what your competences are. Odd bits of paper scattered around the house will not convince anyone of your worth; if you have not already done so start organising from now onwards.

Now and the future
The whole of the NVQ/SVQ philosophy is built around candidates' portfolios. Records of work achieved, curriculum vitae, testimonials, statements by others that certain tasks have been undertaken or skills observed, assessments, photographs showing work done, plans, charts, essays, notes and diaries can all be included.

Validated information
All work in an NVQ/SVQ portfolio needs to be signed and dated to validate the records. Photographs should be signed on the back, witness statements clearly identified by the observer including their status – supervisor, colleague, parent, manager.

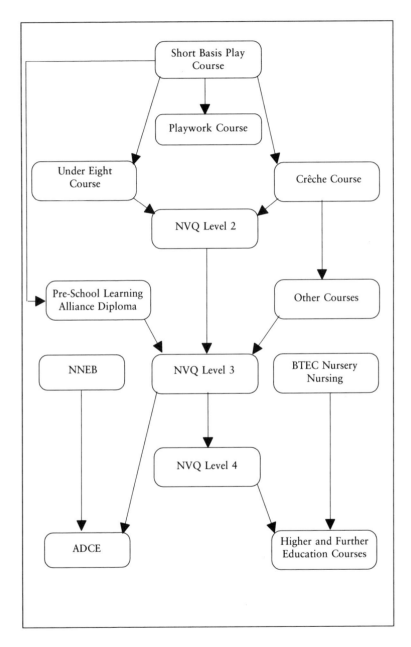

Fig. 7. Some training opportunities.

Identifying relevant experiences
So many experiences occur in the workplace it can sometimes be difficult to decide how much should go in a portfolio. You need to be selective, but what goes in should reflect a range of activities and interactions to represent the complexity of childcare. Some areas will be in greater depth than others. The more occasional situations – an accident, incident, illness, rare occurrence – are the areas you must catch and record because they are difficult to recreate when an assessor is there to observe.

Other training opportunities
- Children's nursing: either through a Diploma of Higher Education in Nursing Studies or a degree in nursing.

- School nurse: Registered General Nurse with an additional School Nursing Diploma.

- Nursery or primary teaching: either through a Bachelor of Education degree, or as a Post Graduate Certificate of Education.

- Degree: under a variety of titles and varying contents – Early Years, Early Childhood Studies, Childhood Studies, Speech and Language Therapy.

- Short courses on specific subjects: these will be presented by and through colleges either as 'one offs' or as a series by one of the professional organisations.

DISCUSSION POINTS

1. Are you willing to commit the time, energy and resources that the right training will demand?

2. How will you go about investigating all the sources of training?

3. Can you expect full support from family and friends if you decide to commit yourself wholly to training?

7
Preparing for the Job Market

PREVIEW

In this chapter we will discuss:

- how to organise your personal information

- raising your awareness of all sources for advertisements/job information

- what equal opportunity means for you

- giving the information required.

COLLECTING FOR A PORTFOLIO

As you start to gain your experience, or take training, be organised in the collection of reports, testimonials, certificates. Prepare yourself with an A4 folder of plastic pockets and arrange information in the order you get it. As you progress, place in it GCSE certificates, first aid certificates, food hygiene certificates, dates and brief outlines of work experience, volunteer work or course placements. Do not wait until you have been invited for an interview before scrambling around to find the information from various tucked away places. Be prepared.

FINDING OUT ABOUT JOBS

Do not be complacent about finding out about jobs: they are unlikely to seek you out, you need to go out and find them. There are a number of places to keep your ears and eyes on.

Scanning the local papers
Many childcare jobs are advertised in local papers, but you may have to search them out. They may appear as part of a corporate advert, as for a local authority, along with other types of jobs. They could be in a block advert referring to childcare specific jobs, or they could be tucked away in the classified. Health authorities might advertise on one particular day in the week, Social Services on another, leisure services on a third, the voluntary and private sector at any time. Take a note of advertising patterns in your local press.

Minority press
It is worth looking for adverts in the minority press, particularly if there are high proportions of ethnic minority people in the community, an under representation in the workforce, and publications specifically aimed at these groups. Limited circulation publications may be in your area: make a point of looking them over.

Visiting the Job Centre
Do not neglect your local Job Centre where childcare jobs, particularly with local authorities, may well be on offer. Discuss your needs with career officers.

Listening to word of mouth
Playgroup and private nursery work is often advertised by word of mouth, keep your ears open. The disadvantage of this approach is that it is not meeting equal opportunities as, for instance, if all the workers are white and they only tell their white friends about vacancies then there is never going to be representation from other ethnic groups. This type of recruitment is not to be encouraged. However, if a group is open for volunteer help and you hear of it and can respond, it could be a useful starting point for you.

Finding authority bulletins
Local authorities, city, borough and county councils, and health authorities may produce a staff vacancy bulletin on a weekly or fortnightly basis. Apart from being circulated among staff they are often displayed in reception areas or libraries. Make contact and seek them out.

Fig. 8. Advertisement sheet.

Studying noticeboards
Community groups may put up vacancy bulletins on noticeboards, particularly when requesting volunteers.

Reading the specialist press/national magazines
For the widest range of jobs in nurseries – with local authorities, Montessori schools, colleges, hospitals, childcare recruitment agencies, and jobs with families – the highest number of advertisements are contained in the weekly magazine *Nursery World*. Private families looking for nannies, mothers helps, maternity nurses, *au pairs*, and agencies recruiting for these posts, appear weekly in *The Lady* magazine. More specialist posts in the health service may be advertised in the monthly nursing magazines.

READING THE ADVERTISEMENT

Know what you are applying for, read the advertisement and job information carefully. A nursery nurse colleague once, long ago, applied for a job in a nursery only to find, to her embarrassment, that it was a plant nursery. Make sure **you** are applying for the right post. Take particular note if a closing date is included and make sure your application is submitted in good time.

Being aware of equal opportunities
It is not unusual to see references to organisations and companies identifying themselves as Equal Opportunity employers. This causes confusion in some people who do not have a clear understanding of what this means for them. We all grow up with certain prejudices, cultural interpretations, and ways of looking at others. Equal opportunities are ways of addressing these issues, ironing out the differences, not discriminating against any particular group or person, being fair to everyone, dealing in facts and not feelings.

What does it mean?
Rather than accepting the first person who knocks on the door looking for work, the job should be advertised, a closing date set, and all applicants given equal consideration. The job should not have unnecessary barriers put in the way which stop people being offered employment. Discrimination against people because they are male/female, gay, black, disabled, have a first language other than English, wear head or leg covering, have children is not

acceptable. Each should be considered on their merits. Can they do the job? It is a positive asset to have staff who can speak the same language as the children, who can show that disabled people can achieve in all areas of work, that black people can be leaders as well as followers, that men can be good childcarers.

Within employment law, however, there are clearly defined exceptions, such as women only to work in a women's refuge, or an Asian worker if that is particularly pertinent to the children being cared for. These are, however, rare exceptions and the relevant section of the Act must appear in the advert. For all applicants the same questions should be asked at application stage, prepared questions used at interview not made up on the spot when you see the candidate, and care taken that questions are not so culturally biased that a sector of the community will be automatically excluded. Minority groups and disabled people can be encouraged to apply by recognising their particular strengths, to redress balances of representation, and to ensure equal opportunities can be adequately addressed in the service delivery. Equal opportunity means the 'best' person should be offered the job.

Monitoring information
You may be asked questions on the application form relating to, particularly, ethnic origin. Do not be alarmed by this, it will not be used to discriminate against you. In fact by monitoring the information the organisation's management can check they are targeting their advertisements towards the right place, that representative samples of people apply and are short-listed, and that job offers are not discriminating against particular groups of people.

Asking for help
Putting in a job application is not an examination, where asking for help is cheating, but an opportunity for you to put into writing what you have done and why you are the right person for the job. If you need assistance ask for it. As long as the information is true someone else can help you write it, particularly if English is not your first language or you are dyslexic.

Being fair to everyone
Recruiters should make short-listing decisions based on the information given. Certainly for childcare assistants, where writing

is not part of the job, it would be discriminatory to exclude people at application stage because they were poor at expressing themselves in writing, or physically getting the words on paper, and not allowing them help. For more senior jobs, if the written word for reports, observations, and administration is a requirement, this could be tested out. Depending on the type and location of the work, colleagues, and clients, customers or patients, certain limitations may be accommodated with support. If you are invited for interview that is the time you will be able to demonstrate your knowledge, ability, and aptitude. Equal opportunities do not mean that any one group of people should have an advantage over another, but that the best person for the job should get it.

CASE STUDY

Darra changes her technique

Job hunting had not been a success for Darra. 'I'd applied for several jobs but all I'd received was a "thank you but no thank you" letter. I couldn't understand why.' There had been a variety of caring posts, nursery assistant, crèche worker, even a supervisor of special needs children on the school run, but Darra had been rather peeved not to have been invited for interview. 'I knew if they met me I would be able to tell them about my experience. Show them my enthusiasm. I was sure I could do it. But I didn't get that far. It was so demoralising.' Then Darra met up again with Mary whom she had not seen since they had gone their separate ways to different colleges, she to do Community Care and Mary to a BTEC course. Mary had a really interesting job as an assistant in an assessment centre.

Mary explained how she had undertaken an assignment on her course on 'getting that first job'. She talked through her experiences with Darra: like reading the information carefully, noting what specific training and experiences were being asked for, and giving the relevant information on the application form. She had to apply for three jobs before being offered one, but had been interviewed each time and that had given her valuable experience as well. It paid off because on the third occasion she had been lucky, or was it just she was the best candidate.

Darra took note of the advice and when a job was advertised at a school across town she put in an application and this time was invited for interview. She didn't get the job first time round, but when it unexpectedly became vacant again a few weeks later they called her back in and offered her the job. 'It was the best news I could ever hear,' she grinned. 'I must ring Mary up and thank her. Without her advice I could have been floundering forever without knowing why.'

WRITING THE LETTER OF APPLICATION

Different employers favour different ways of applying for jobs. Some will only accept application forms, others will want a letter of application, some a CV, others will want a combination of approaches. Take note of what the advertiser/employer is asking of you: if they say 'CVs not required' then you know you have to get all the information on the application form. If you are asked to send a letter of application in your own handwriting then give yourself plenty of time to do it, draft it first on scrap paper then copy it out carefully. Remember this is the first impression the potential employer has of you. If you send a CV make it a good one.

Writing the CV

A curriculum vitae is a concise record of your professional and academic life, your work experiences and interests. It is not intended to be a book, but a list of items, facts which give the recruiter an outline of your achievements (see Figure 9).

Tips to help you
1. Keep it to one, or at most two sides of A4 paper.
2. Make sure it's well presented, clean and uncrumpled.
3. Get it word processed and easy to read.
4. Check spelling is correct.
5. Start with your most recent experience/training.
6. Record the items most relevant to the work.
7. Outside interests make you look a more rounded person.
8. Be positive, make it look good, be truthful.
9. Print it on pale coloured paper if you can to make it stand out.
10. Check that your referees are happy to be contacted.

CURRICULUM VITAE

Name: Rajinder Kaur

Address: 257 Dovedale Avenue, Normanton, Derby

Telephone No: 01987 654 321

Date of Birth: 24.12.75

Education/Training: Fullstead College, Renwick
NNEB 1994–1996
BTEC Community Care 1991–1993
Holbrook Hall School 1986–1991
GCSE in English C French B
Maths D Geography B
Art C Biology C

Professional Experience: Nursery Assistant Medina Nursery – 1996–present
Family grouping – 18 months to 5 years

Placements on NNEB:
Tingdale Primary School–
5-year-olds
One Two Nursery School–
2 to 5-year-olds
Holbrook Hospital –
Children's ward
Neat Day Nursery –
3 months to 2 years

Care Assistant – Rose Aster Special School 1993–1994

Fig. 9. Sample CV.

	Personal care of 10 year old disabled child
	Placements on Community Care Course: Roundhill Playgroup – 3 to 5-year-olds Netherfield Elderly Persons Home Red Cross shop
Personal Qualities:	Enthusiastic, confident, committed, caring, speak Punjabi. Special interests art, crafts and music.
Hobbies:	Art, swimming, badminton, Punjabi music.
Referees:	Mrs D Shah Telephone – 571257 Medina Nursery 11 Merton Road Renwick
	Mr F Smith Telephone – 887235 45 The Terrace Trington

Fig. 9. Sample CV (*cont.*).

Questions and Answers

When I am looking for a job must I always wait to see something advertised before I contact organisations?

No, it is always worth letting people know you are interested. Sometimes you will strike lucky and they may come back to you with information on what's on offer, other times you may be told to look out for the adverts. However, if you are keen to gain experience you may be offered voluntary work which will put you in a stronger position when a job comes up. In fact being on the 'inside' may mean you hear about jobs which you might otherwise have missed. Having some insider knowledge of how a particular type of provision functions may make it easier for you to complete an application form when the opportunity comes. So even if there is nothing going at that point contacting a potential employer may pay off in the long term.

I am a veiled Muslim woman. I can take the veil off in an all female environment, but would not be comfortable working with men. Is there any chance of my getting a job?

The working restrictions you have mean you will have to pick your locations carefully, but you certainly should be able to find suitable employment. When you make an application tell them you wear a veil and ask for an all women interview panel. If you are short-listed discuss in what circumstances you can and cannot work and then if you are offered work it can be on the terms discussed. You are perhaps fortunate in your chosen career in that it is dominated by women, both as colleagues and users. Women's centres with childcare facilities would be an obvious choice, but general childcare provision might be suitable if you removed your veil for the children, adjusting it when parents collected their children and fathers were present. There are, of course, likely to be men using public service buildings and you will need to be prepared for this.

APPLYING FOR THE JOB

Applications need to be tackled intelligently and truthfully, although the technique is to give appropriate information to fulfill the requirements, and to play down weak spots. See Figure 10 for an example of an application form.

Respecting the guidance
A number of organisations will provide information and advice to prospective applicants to enable them to understand the requirements of the job, details regarding the application, and knowledge of the process of recruitment. To improve your chances of being offered a job you **must** read and apply the guidance.

Job description
With most jobs a job description will be supplied on application. This will identify the main purpose of the job, the major objectives, and summaries of tasks expected to be undertaken. Assess your skills and experiences against this and refer to them in your application.

Person specification
This is not a familiar term to many people, but it is just a way of saying what experience, training, awareness and attitudes are hoped for in the person who will be offered the job. Many organisations will prepare them to choose who will be interviewed, some will supply them with the application form (see Figure 11). If you are sent a person specification read it carefully – it is an important document. If it says it is essential to have had certain experiences, skills, or training you must put those of your own experiences, skills and training that fit those requirements in the application, otherwise you risk not being short-listed. If it says certain aspects such as abilities and attitudes are to be tested at interview then you can expect to be asked questions to confirm those. It helps you prepare for the recruitment process.

Filling in the application form
Make sure the completed form:

- is neat and tidy

- is fully filled in

- includes sufficient information to meet the person specification

- is accurate

LITTLE BOXES NURSERY, BAY GREEN, KENT

APPLICATION FORM

1 Mr/Mrs/Ms/Miss	2 Surname	3 First Names

4 Address

5 Present Employer

6 Qualification/Training

7 Previous Employment

8 Information in support of your application

9 Monitoring Information   I am –   Male ❑   Female ❑
     African Caribbean ❑   Asian ❑   White ❑   Other ❑

10 Hobbies

11 Names and Addresses of Two Referees

12 Signature ....   Date.........................

Fig. 10. Example of an application form.

		WIDEAWAKE CRECHE BROOM STREET OAKHAM

POST: CRECHE ASSISTANT   RATE £4.79 HOUR

PERSON SPECIFICATION   POST No A/123
E = Essential   D = Desirable

Category	E/D	Criteria	Test method
SKILLS KNOWLEDGE and EXPERIENCE	E	Experience of working with under 5s in groups	Application form and Interview
	D	Experience with under 2s	Application form and Interview
	D	Awareness of needs of disabled children	Interview
EQUAL OPPORTUNITY	E	Understanding of anti-sexist play	Interview
	E	Awareness of play needs of children from ethnic minority backgrounds	Interview
	D	Able to speak a second language	Application form and Interview
QUALIFICATIONS	E	Under 5 course	Application form and Interview
ATTITUDE and MOTIVATION	E	Non-judgemental	Interview
	E	Caring and understanding	Interview
	E	Able to work as part of a team	Interview
	E	Able to work hours required	Interview
OTHER			

Fig. 11. Example of a person specification.

- presents the positive

- gives the names of referees who are available for quick responses.

Answering the questions

The recruiter can only know what training you have done, what your experiences are, what your skills and interests are if you tell them. Use your opportunity wisely. Read the questions carefully, give as full a response as you can without waffling. If you have been given a person specification make sure you write in your experiences which apply to the expectations; this way you will increase your chances of being invited to an interview where you can use your personality and powers of persuasion.

Points to remember

Only you can get yourself a job ultimately, but others can help.

- Be efficient at collecting and presenting your certificates, reports *etc*. Talk to others to identify what should go in your portfolio.

- Tell as many people as possible what sort of job you are looking for and pick up the contacts. Keep well informed.

- Familiarise yourself with equal opportunity issues so you understand what they mean to yourself, employees, service users, and the children likely to be in your care.

- Learn the techniques of applying for a job, practise writing information in a readable manner without waffling. Ask contacts to advise you to give yourself confidence with the real thing.

DISCUSSION POINTS

1. Who do you know who could help you if needed with your applications?

2. If your handwriting isn't very legible, is there anything you can do to improve it?

3. Have you contacted potential referees to make sure they are willing to help you?

8
Getting Through the Interview

PREVIEW

In this chapter we will cover:

- giving yourselves plenty of time to get ready and get there

- learning to relax and go in smiling

- answering the questions as carefully and fully as possible

- asking questions about the job, conditions, anything you do not understand

- waiting hopefully.

PREPARING FOR THE BIG DAY

Instead of being overwhelmed by the thought of an interview take it one step at a time, and be well prepared.

Dressing for the part

Attending an interview is an event not to be taken lightly. Prepare yourself well, get a good night's sleep, choose and lay out your clothes the night before if the interview is early, and 'think smart'. The important thing is to be comfortable but clean and well groomed. Make sure your shoes are clean and polished. You are not applying for the chief executive post so no one expects you to bankrupt yourself to buy designer clothes and Gucci shoes. Just wear your smartest clothes; go with freshly washed, tidy hair. First impressions **are** important.

Knowing where you are going

Make sure you know where you have to be for the interview. If you are not sure make a trial run at around the same time you are expected, to assess how long it takes you; then you will not be late on the day. Give yourself plenty of time, allow 15 minutes beforehand to settle yourself down, go to the toilet, have a coffee if offered, read any information which may be given to you. There is nothing worse than arriving with seconds to spare, feeling hot and flustered, and not having time to gather your thoughts.

Packing your bag

At least the day before make sure you have located any certificates you have, and they are presented logically in a folder. Re-read your interview letter and any information received. If it asks for evidence of working with children select photographs you can talk about, craft work you have done with them, testimonials or placement assessment sheets, and package them neatly in plastic pockets in a ring binder or in a box file. Be selective and choose the most positive and interesting pieces. Do not take too much, there will not be much time to talk about your portfolio, and you are likely to be asked questions about the contents so think through what you will say.

Questions and Answers

I have been advised to wear a suit when I go for an interview. However, I always wear leggings, jeans or trousers and I feel uncomfortable wearing a skirt. Is it really necessary?

The clothes you are expected to wear for an interview are, to a degree, reflective of the job you are going for. If it's chief executive you want then leggings are definitely out! However, for childcare jobs most interviewers are more liberal, expecting you to wear clean well cared for clothes which would be suitable for the work. Jeans are better left at home. Having an interview can be quite an ordeal, so choose your clothes carefully: if you feel you look your best it will free you up to concentrate on other aspects. Bearing in mind that overall impressions are important and you will be competing against others, your actual choice of clothes will depend on your wardrobe and budget. Extremes are better left for some more social occasion when there is less at stake.

As I have a special interest and personal experience of disabled children – my little brother has cerebral palsy – I would like to tell the interviewers about this. What if they don't ask me a specific question about this area, can I still tell them?

Certainly, you would be doing yourself a great disservice if you omitted this information. If you listen carefully to the questions you may well find one or more will give you the opportunity to introduce this subject. You are most likely to be asked about your experience with children, probably the first question, and here is one chance. Alternatively if you are asked about equal opportunities you will be able to make reference to the needs of disabled children and how these could be met. If you are not able to pick up the reference on these occasions, wait until you are asked what skills or experiences you have to offer, or if there is anything you want to add: tell of your interest and experience then. Having such personal experience is very valuable, particularly if you are able to relate it to other children, their parents, and the impact on the rest of the family. Use all your assets to get yourself that job!

KNOWING WHAT TO EXPECT

Pre-interview preparations

Find out as much as you can about the organisation, provision and job you have applied for. You may have been sent general information, notes on anything from filling in the application form, equal opportunities, or need for police checks, job description, and/or person specification, when you applied for the job. Read it thoroughly. If you are not clear about any elements either ring up the contact given and clarify the point, or save up the question for the interview. If no indication is given that you will have an opportunity to look around the provision ask if you can do so beforehand or on the day of the interview. Write down any questions you have in a notebook and take it with you to the interview; no one will mind and it will emphasise the point that you have taken the trouble to consider the issues carefully. Interviews should be a two way process with you finding out what would be expected of you, and the interviewers finding out if you are the person they are looking for.

What will it be like?

You can expect two people whom you will be working with, perhaps the manager or leader, interviewing you. It is likely to be fairly formal. You should be introduced to the interviewers, welcomed, told what to expect during the interview, advised when it would be appropriate for you to ask questions. At the end you should be given conditions of the job and told when and how you can expect to hear. You should expect the interview to take place in an office and wise recruiters will have a 'Do not disturb' notice on the door and have the telephone barred so there are no interruptions.

The interviewers want to get the best out of you so they will try to make you feel as comfortable as possible, knowing that for most people interviews are quite an ordeal. Do not be alarmed if the interviewers make notes as you go through the interview – it does not mean you have said something wrong, it's just to remind them what you have said when they come to make the decisions afterward. Some recruiters will not write anything down while you are in the room, but will record responses immediately after the interview. You should be told how and when you can expect to hear the outcome before you leave; if you are not told, ask.

Taking deep breaths

Few people are not nervous when attending interviews. You can take some steps to help you through the process:

- Find out as much about the job as you can beforehand.

- Prepare a list of questions.

- Be sure you know how to get to the interview location.

- Arrive 15 minutes before time.

- Keep calm – taking deep breaths helps.

- Go into the interview with confidence – saying to yourself 'I can and I **will**'.

BEING READY FOR THE QUESTIONS

When you are invited into the interview take a big breath, go confidently, smile at the interviewers, sit comfortably on the chair you are directed to. If you are wearing a coat, and it is warm, it will make you feel more comfortable if you lay it on a convenient chair, or behind you. Decide if you feel better sitting with your portfolio on your lap or placing it on the floor. It looks awkward if you hold it, but some people feel more secure if they have something to hang on to. Take a couple more big breaths and you are ready for off.

Taking your time

When asked a question listen carefully. Take your time, there is no need to rush the answer out. If you are not sure if you heard the whole of the question ask for it to be repeated. If you do not understand what is being asked say so. Say 'I don't quite understand, please can you rephrase the question?' To give yourself more thinking time when asked a question, repeat it aloud to yourself. If you have not answered as fully as you might you can expect to have supplementary questions asked, or short prompts – 'tell us some more about that', 'and what else?', 'is there anything else?' Good interview questions will be 'open' *ie* will require more than a yes/no answer. Many will be sufficiently broad ranging to enable you to give a range of responses, so if you forget some aspect in one reply you may be able to pop it in another.

Making no assumptions

No matter what your previous experience, knowledge of the recruiters and they of you, in an interview situation you will need to explain everything. Do not make assumptions that because it is known you have an NNEB or PLA Diploma, or the interviewers have seen you working, or whatever, that you have no need to fully answer questions – that 'they will already know'. They may not, or may not be able to use that outside knowledge under the terms of equality of opportunity. Assume that the person asking the question has never met you, knows nothing about you, knows nothing about courses and their content, and little about childcare and related subjects, and give full responses. Remember you are in a competitive market, it is up to you to sell yourself. The key to success is being prepared.

Agreeing the conditions

You should be given information on the conditions applicable to the job: hours, annual salary or hourly rate, details of superannuation, probationary period, holiday entitlement. If it has not been supplied to you in writing beforehand, or been given orally outside the interview, you can expect to be given the details at the end of the interview. If nothing is said it is quite legitimate for you to ask these questions before you leave. However, if you forget, or are not given, any particular piece of information you will be able to clarify this at the time of offer, should you be successful. Make sure you are happy with the conditions before saying yes, as once you have accepted you are likely to be committed to them. You may not be seen very favourably if you accept, start work, and then say you want things changed. Better to get things sorted out beforehand; at least then if they cannot be changed you will know what you are taking on.

CASE STUDY

Vernice finds that preparation pays off

Vernice had been for three interviews, so she had gained a bit of experience on different recruiter styles. She recognised that nerves and inexperience had got the better of her on those occasions. 'I felt I was now ready to have a real go at getting the job,' she said as the invitation came to interview for a playworker. Vernice knew the job was with a voluntary organisation so she made enquiries to find out as much as she could before the big day. She had followed advice and prepared her portfolio with details of work experience, certificates, photographs of displays she had done with the children, and her CV. 'I hadn't any money to buy new clothes, but washed and pressed my blouse and skirt, polished my boots and laid them out ready for morning.'

Giving herself plenty of time the morning of the interview she showered and washed her hair. Feeling good about herself, she felt, was one of the aspects which would see her through with confidence. She knew she looked good. When she arrived for the interview she found two other candidates also hoping for the job. Vernice found this a bit disconcerting. The others seemed so confident, she felt they had more experience than her. 'They were bragging about where they had worked. I don't know where one of them had her certificates and evidence but she was only carrying a tiny bag. The other one didn't seem to mind that she had a coffee stain on her leggings and scuffed boots.'

Feeling she had nothing to lose, and yet another interview would just give her a bit more experience, Vernice went in smiling. Because she was more relaxed the interview seemed to go well, she answered the questions as well as she could, and came out feeling good. Not surprisingly the following week Vernice received what she had been waiting for – the offer letter. 'I think it was because I had taken the trouble to be prepared,' she said, 'and I also think I had the positive attitude they were looking for.'

The sort of questions you might be asked
1. Tell us about your experience with under fives to date.
2. Which of your course placements did you most enjoy?
3. What do you understand by the term equal opportunity?
4. How would you expect to see equal opportunities implemented in the nursery?
5. Imagine you have a two-year-old in your care who keeps biting other children. How would you prevent this from happening? Why do you think children behave in this way?
6. What can you suggest to help settle a child in?
7. If you were the leader and the alarms sounded what would you need to consider? How would you organise an evacuation?
8. If you are working with a nursery officer who wants to work in a different way to you how would you set about resolving the conflict?

WHAT HAPPENS NEXT

Making the decisions
Following the interviews the recruiters will need to consider all the candidates in order to decide who should be selected. Because they have asked the same questions of everyone, and made notes of their responses, they will be able to compare one candidate with another. The one who came over with the most appropriate answers, the right attitude, suitable experience, leadership abilities, team qualities, perhaps additional factors like special skills, greater cultural awareness, knowledge of disability issues, *etc* will be

deemed to be the 'best' candidate and offered the job. You may be telephoned with the result or have to wait for a letter.

The final hurdles

- If they have not already been sent for references will be taken up at this stage.

- You will be checked out medically, which could mean attending for a medical examination, filling in a form, or your GP being contacted.

- Personal statement forms for Social Services clearance under the Children Act 1989 will need to be completed.

- Police check form will need to be filled in.

- You may be asked to start work before the clearances come through, subject to them being satisfactory.

- In some instances you will not be able to start work before all the clearances have been completed.

Step-by-step summary
1. Prepare yourself for the interview.
2. Go into the interview with confidence.
3. A positive result.
4. All the clearance checks will need to be made.
5. Start the new job.
6. Congratulations!

SEEKING ADVICE OR COUNSELLING

Looking to the future
If you have applied for promotion or an alternative job with your current employer and are unsuccessful it would be in your interests to ask why so that you can better prepare yourself for next time. It may be very straightforward – that someone else had heaps more experience than you, or very specific experience they wanted that you did not have; or it might have been your technique which let you down, or your presentation, or your lack of awareness in a

particular area. Some things only time can address, but for others you can help yourself if you know what they are. Some organisations have a policy of counselling unsuccessful candidates, if they want it, particularly internal applicants but sometimes external if they enquire. Take advantage of this because it may point you in a particular direction, to improve your technique, towards a course or reading material, or spur you into action to gain experience in a certain area where a gap is identified. The alternative is that you flounder around, feeling a failure for not getting the job you want, after being regularly rejected after interview. The remedy is in your hands.

DISCUSSION POINTS

1. What do you think is most likely to worry you about preparing for an interview? What can you do to counter it?

2. What materials can you put in your portfolio?

3. Is there anyone you know who could give you a mock interview for practice?

9
Getting the Best out of the Job

PREVIEW

In this chapter we will help you with:

- using your colleagues to develop your own experiences
- finding your role in the provision
- valuing on-going training within the work situation
- knowing when it's time to take further courses.

LEARNING FROM OTHERS

Having successfully negotiated the tough rounds of application and selection, once you get into post you should not sit back and be complacent: there is a whole lot more to do and to learn to do.

Taking note of the experienced

As a newcomer to childcare you will undoubtedly start your career by being the most junior member in the provision. Use the position wisely, learn from your colleagues. Notice what they do, question why, ask if you can try ideas out. If you do not understand something ask, have a thirst for knowledge, read childcare magazines and books, be prepared to learn outside work hours. However, a word of warning – be sensitive to others, if you drive people mad with your questions you will not endear yourself to them.

Carrying on learning

Training courses, workshops, seminars and conferences take place all over the country all the time. Take advantage of them. Just because you have completed a substantial childcare course does not mean you know everything. At an appropriate time ask your employer to nominate you for any in-service or external training as it becomes available. Keep a look out for any interesting presentations you may be able to attend; do not wait for or expect others always to do it for you. Eventually you could be the one person in the workplace to specialise in one particular area, developing expertise, advising others, supporting your colleagues, and giving yourself an edge over others when it comes to promotion.

DEVELOPING RELATIONSHIPS

Getting the most out of experiences

Working in childcare demands a degree of socialisation which may be less well developed in some other professions. You have to talk to children and colleagues, be prepared to 'perform' (as in story telling, singing, or dressing up) and plan and share ideas together. Not only do you need theoretical knowledge, but you have to be a good team player too. Each member of staff working mechanically, but in isolation, does not make for good quality provision. By working together so much more can be achieved. There is likely to be a range of levels and varieties of experiences within the staff team which can be called on to extend the knowledge and practice of newly appointed childcarers. Developing relationships fosters the supportive approach required. Make the most of your colleagues.

Questions and answers

Having qualified as a nursery nurse four years ago I have, until now, been very satisfied with my role. However, I now feel I should be thinking about my future. How can I help myself?

Be prepared to take responsibility if you are given the opportunity. Offer to take new staff under your wing, be prepared to organise trips, introduce ideas for training sessions into team meetings and agree to lead them if you have the expertise, suggest new methods of monitoring or changes to forms, cover for absent senior staff, speak up at team meetings, show parents and visitors around. If you have childcare students in the establishment perhaps you could be responsible for one, guiding, advising, supervising, writing assessment reports. It will good experience for you and useful to have on your CV.

As a move on in your personal development consider additional training to update your knowledge, building on four years of experience. If you can gain support from your employer for day release the Advanced Diploma in Childcare and Education would give you opportunities to meet with colleagues from a variety of other settings, sharing ideas, stretching you, and perhaps helping formulate a career path to aim at.

I am particularly interested in working with children with communication problems: we have two in our nursery who need special help. What can I do which will help me in my work and also benefit the children?

Find out as much about the care of the children as you can. Ask if you can talk with any professionals visiting the children, get involved in the care and development programme, become one of the 'specialists' in your nursery. Follow this up with attendance at conferences and seminars on the subject, even if it's your own time and expense. Take the trouble to learn Makaton, if that's an appropriate communication system, British Sign Language, or use the phonic ear. Share your knowledge and skills with your colleagues *and* the other children. If your children are surrounded by a variety of communication methods they will quickly pick up the basics. Develop methods of communicating, story telling, group work, which includes all children. Encourage your colleagues to write an Inclusive Play Policy.

The interests of the children and the harmony of the nursery are better met if everyone is following the same guidelines, particularly if drawn up by themselves rather than imposed by managers. You will then find greater satisfaction in your work, will have the additional rewards of seeing the children develop, and be instrumental in adding a new dimension to the nursery. This experience could also be the first step towards the future: you can add it to your CV, specialise in this area of nursery work, seek employment as a nursery nurse in this specialised field, or go on to train as a speech therapist or teacher of the deaf.

PRACTISING YOUR SKILLS

Many opportunities exist to develop skills in childcare settings, whatever they are, as long as you are prepared to commit yourself.

Collecting your evidence

Do not lose or waste particular experiences, save evidence as it evolves; it is much easier than trying to remember what you did when. Make notes of interesting projects you have undertaken with the children, take photographs to remind you. Keep conference programmes, training course outlines you have attended. Record moves from one area of work to another, baby room, pre-school group, rising fives, out-of-school. All of this will be useful for you when you come to reassess your career in readiness to move on.

Developing within disability

Many wrongly assume disabled people cannot work in childcare. It is true that in the past opportunities offered for training have been few, but with a more enlightened outlook the future should be more positive for disabled students. Depending on the disability, childcarers with that added perspective can be a great asset to the provision. Hearing impaired childcarers can quickly spot a lip reading child others may have missed. For parents of a disabled child, an adult able to demonstrate a professional position on an equal basis with all others is a valuable role model. Many disabilities are no impairment at all. A disabled member of staff should not be singled out to be the spokesperson for all issues around disability unless they want to. However, in general discussions on childcare issues the disabled member of staff can give a pertinent perspective to benefit all children. When further or in-service training is being allocated disabled people should be considered for the full range, giving them the opportunity to develop areas of specialism or readiness for promotion as for any other employee.

CASE STUDY

Ilona gets herself noticed

Working for a local authority gave Ilona the opportunity to consolidate her training. 'I took advantage of everything I was offered,' she said, 'and it really paid off.' She gained experience working with the children, became a mentor to less experienced staff, and over time started to 'act up' when the opportunity came. Because she was always willing to participate, was reliable and committed, the Officer-in-Charge quickly recognised her potential. 'Because some of my colleagues were reluctant to put themselves forward I found I was being nominated, particularly, for health and safety type in-service training.' With this knowledge Ilona was able to draw up a health and safety policy with her colleagues, took responsibility for organising the storage of equipment with regard to staff safety, and devised safety awareness programmes with the children.

'I didn't expect to move into this area,' she confided, 'but when it happened I found I quite enjoyed it.' First aid and basic food hygiene followed. 'Before I knew it I was the specialist in the centre. It sounds like a dull subject, but it's not. The more I found out the more I discovered there was to learn.' Because of her enthusiasm other members of staff became enthusiastic. 'At a team meeting someone suggested a project on teeth, a brainstorming produced masses of ideas, from the dentist chair, giant toothbrush and paste, talks to the parents, leaflets from Health Promotion, to reassessing routines for teeth cleaning to ensure a less rushed job. It became a really satisfying area of work with long term benefits.'

This early extension into working with parents led on to Ilona taking an adult teaching certificate, and found herself really attracted to this area of work. When a job came up in the Health Promotion team for a Home Safety Officer Ilona was able to apply with a degree of confidence which surprised even her. 'It was only because I said yes to everything that I found myself in this position. When I took my initial childcare training I never expected to end up here. But I did,' she smiled, 'and it's the most satisfying job in the world, getting the message across to parents and carers how important safety is for their children.'

TAKING ADVANTAGE OF IN-SERVICE TRAINING

Missing no opportunities

Training can come in many forms: formally through a certificated course, informally by working alongside others – *ie* coaching, workshops, short courses, in-service training, intra-team presentations. In-service training can support many aspects of your work, not just directly childcare related. Take advantage of it all. It may be health and safety, recruitment and selection, leadership, manual handling, food hygiene, supervision, first aid, personal development, computer usage, presentation skills.

Valuing all training
When, in the interests of a new job or promotion, it comes to listing the training you have received do not ignore any elements. If you have taken advantage of say a two-hour a month in-service training session make reference to this. Over a period of years this can amount to a substantial amount of training, particularly if you can show how you put it into practice. Because it is not certificated does not mean you should undervalue any of it. If you have been able to present any training to your colleagues this will indicate your level of knowledge and expertise. An accumulation of many short courses, two hours to four days or whatever, can add substantially to your list of accomplishments.

Gathering all this information together can be particularly valuable if you do not have a substantial recognised childcare qualification. On such occasions when jobs are advertised as NNEB or equivalent if you are able to put down any courses you have done, plus all the in-service training you have undertaken, it may just get you that interview so that you can demonstrate to the recruiters your competence. Without it you may never get the chance.

SEEKING FURTHER TRAINING

Backing up your position
Strong as your skills and experiences may be in the 'hands-on' childcare aspects, in order to develop your career you will need to consider other training which will prepare you for opportunities as they arise. Some areas to cover:

- all round awareness of issues revolving around the provision

- leadership skills

- planning and organisation skills

- recruitment and selection knowledge and skills
- counselling skills
- budget management skills
- supervisory skills
- staff appraisal techniques
- updating of childcare issues
- staff training techniques
- conducting meetings.

Moving into management

Opportunities exist for those who are prepared to move into management. All round training from a selection of different perspectives – community childcare, babies, sick children, Social Services, special needs, education, training, school age children, assessment – will increase awareness necessary for the more general managerial roles. Take the initiative and develop your own action plan for progress. Competition for jobs is great, be ready for the challenge.

Points to remember

Gaining a job is only the first step: developing it, getting satisfaction, and making a career of it require commitment and effort.

- Discuss with your colleagues their areas of experience and special interest.

- Assess your workplace and identify any gaps you might be interested to fill. Discuss this with your manager; consider relevant training you might undertake either in the workplace or outside, in work time or your own.

- Do not turn down any opportunity for learning, especially if you want to move into new and interesting areas of work.

- Nothing of value comes without effort. Give yourself three targets for achievement in the next year.

DISCUSSION POINTS

1. Are there particular areas in which you would like to specialise?

2. Would you be prepared to pay for your own further training?

3. What might hinder you from moving into management?

10
Moving On

PREVIEW

In this chapter we will look at:

- considering the options

- moving through the system

- managing in management.

BEING ALERT TO FURTHER OPPORTUNITIES

Once qualified and with the necessary experience many consider it time to move on – but to where? There are six potential options: sideways, upwards, or outwards within your own organisation, or in another. Consider each carefully. A **sideways** move would be into a job at the same level as you are at but with a different role: *ie* crêche assistant to play assistant, similar level of responsibilities with new challenges. **Upwards** would mean promotion: nursery officer to deputy manager perhaps. **Outwards** would mean moving to another section or department and could be senior nursery officer to home safety officer, or nursery manager to women's hostel manager.

The advantages of moving within the organisation you know are just that, you know the culture and expectations, you have more idea what to expect, you would not have a break in service, you have knowledge of training opportunities, and they know you. However, you may feel you know all you want to and would like to face the challenges of different structures, the unknown, and additional opportunities. Sometimes you may have no choice in that the opportunities are not present in the place you work. It could be simply that by moving you can earn more money.

Giving it a try
Do not be afraid to try things, career prospects are greater for those who have more experience to offer. Even relatively short periods of experience, across a spectrum of different types of provision, will give useful insight into the needs and demands of an extended range of parents, children and employers.

Ears to the grapevine
If you have been keeping up to date with issues and opportunities around childcare, you will no doubt be aware of developments as they arise in your area. If a new centre is being opened, or you hear of an extension to a nursery, or a voluntary organisation starts a new service, or a health authority focuses on new support for parents, you need not only to take note but also take action. Make contact, express your interest, apply for jobs.

Developing your specialisms
Different types of provision and different agencies will have varying expectations of the staff. Be prepared. All round experience over a range of ages and settings, demonstration of taking responsibility and meeting standards are to be applauded, but in such a competitive field as childcare those having that little bit extra will be the winners. Having a thorough understanding of equal opportunities in action, the curriculum and key stage 0, British Sign language, presentation and training skills, and other such laudable subjects will enable you to have more choice.

Questions and Answers
Having worked for several years in a number of different settings, I'm getting quite interested in management issues. I never really thought about it before, but now I realise there are techniques and styles to handling meetings, managing staff, ensuring the smooth running of the provision. I thought it just happened. Now I'd like to find out more, what areas should I be exploring?

Management can be taught and practised. Once your awareness is raised you will keep noticing different aspects, ways of doing things, differences among staff on how they handle situations.

Discuss your interest with your manager at appraisal meetings, see if coaching could be offered, could you lead a team meeting, or tackle some management issues? Borrow books from your workplace or the public library and read about styles and techniques. Investigate courses – they range from one day seminars on specific aspects, a management focused module in the Advanced Diploma in Childcare and Education, short courses on particular styles like Action Centred Leadership presented by the Industrial Society, NVQ level 3 in Supervisory Studies, Certificate and Diploma in Management Studies, to degrees. The more prepared you are when the opportunity comes for using your skills the better.

Wherever you work these days there seems to be change. My authority has one review after another, reorganisation after reorganisation, greater expectations of the staff. Help, what can I do?

You are quite right in (a) there are a lot of changes happening in all areas of work and (b) it is very positive that you are asking what you can do to minimise the effects and maximise your own position. There is no longer a place for the traditionalist who says, 'I've always done it this way and I don't intend to change.' Not all change is bad. Sometimes it is only by trying new working methods that we can ascertain whether they will work to our advantage or not. In childcare certain aspects must be maintained *eg* staffing ratios and compliance with registration requirements, but working practices must be continually reviewed and updated. So it goes with management. Everyone is looking for value for money, often more senior managers take on a wider remit which entails alterations to the reporting structures, budgets are cut and we need to manage a high quality service on less, and different expectations arise on how reports are presented, who does what, and a greater understanding of the issues required.

Accepting that changes will take place the answer to your question is 'do not be left behind'. Instead of waiting for change to be imposed on you consider all issues and make your own suggestions. If you know budget cuts are coming look where savings can be made and, at the appropriate time, suggest those rather than have something unacceptable imposed. Prepare yourself and your team. Look at creative ways of gaining training in areas which may let you down. Be open minded, see opportunities rather than threats. Above all be positive, you are much more likely to be favoured when change comes than the negative person who moans, is reluctant, or digs in their heels.

TRAVELLING THE HIERARCHY

Moving through the system
There are only two things which stop you moving through the system: your own lack of desire, or lack of appropriate training. If you are happy with your position then good luck, stay there and enjoy it. However, if you want new and challenging experiences, then self-development, maybe taking risks in your career moves, keeping stimulated, continually learning through a variety of processes, being alert to opportunity, and creating your own chances will help you to move from basic to top tier in your chosen profession.

Inexperienced to in-charge
Many a newly qualified nursery nurse will have the ambition eventually to run, or even own, their own nursery. Nothing but hard work, experience and continual updating and extension of knowledge will enable you to be the Officer-in-Charge. To own and run a nursery requires all that and more:

- a great deal of money
- a business plan
- premises
- planning permission
- knowledge of the law related to staff
- health and safety legislation
- and courage.

Seminars on setting up your own nursery are presented from time to time. This may be at specialist exhibitions, advertised by private consultancies, or offered by current owners who choose to share experiences with others. Your local Social Services, who are responsible for registration, may have a pack for sale which will give details of the requirements under the Children Act 1989 and local regulations. It is worth studying this before committing yourself too far.

CASE STUDY

Annie moves into management

'When I left school I knew I wanted to work with children,' said Annie, 'but I hadn't appreciated the satisfaction it was to give me over the years.' Being accepted on the NNEB course gave a good foundation for what was to follow, consolidation by working in school nursery, day nurseries, hospitals and with new born babies. Nursing sick children and midwifery added to the range – conception to adult, in sickness and in health. 'My own children came along and I became involved in what you might call community childcare – childminding, playgroup, parent and toddler group, story telling sessions, and leading on to tutoring playgroup courses.' When her youngest started school Annie was ready for a new challenge and the opportunity came along for a pre-school adviser with Social Services, responsible for registering groups and individuals. 'That was satisfying for a few years before I felt ready for new experiences.'

With a relevant degree now, teaching childcare at an FE college added a new dimension. 'I had little excursions out into "hands on" care occasionally – disabled children, crêche work, nursery supply – just to keep my hand in. You need to know what you're talking about. You cannot afford to lose sight of the children.' Moving on into organising provision was the next stage. 'I took a Masters degree in management, bolted on to childcare aspects, which led me to management proper. Lots of enthusiastic people to work with, exciting opportunities for developing provision, and setting the standards for others. I do believe you have to keep up to date with issues, when you think you know it all it's time to leave, you need to value others and give them recognition for their skills, and you have to share expertise.'

Even after all these years Annie is as enthusiastic about her subject as ever. 'I still have a lot to give, maybe there's another challenge still awaiting me. I do hope so.'

DEVELOPMENTAL TRAINING

Rounding your skills
You will now be aware that from your initial childcare course there are many more avenues and opportunities for you to explore. Some are extensions of the regular mainstream areas, others will take you into new areas, yet more are only peripheral but can become equally absorbing in perhaps a narrower professional field. From time to time you need to take stock of aspects of your current career and consider where your interests lie, and in which direction you may wish to travel.

Ready for opportunities
Suggestions, alternative forms of working with children, and relevant training opportunities are scattered throughout this book. A few additional thoughts are included below.

NVQ assessor
As a practitioner in the workplace a useful development of your own skills, and those of your provision, would be to become a workbased NVQ assessor. You need to be experienced enough to recognise good practice, to be able to question and assess responses, and be able to commit time to undertaking this task. Assessors, like candidates, must be able to demonstrate their competences, show they have knowledge of the process of assessment, be able to produce evidence, and present a portfolio to the awarding body. Usually you attend a few days at a college or assessment centre for training, with on site assessment of the assessor assessing the candidate. The award given is D32 to enable you to assess at level 2, and D33 for level 3. With a D34 you can become an internal verifier.

Ofsted inspector
Suitably experienced and qualified individuals may be recruited to assess whether provision for four-year-olds meets government standards. Advertisements are place in relevant publications when

appropriate. Training is given, and work offered on occasions throughout the year through contractors.

Degrees
Relevant degrees, either first or higher, will not only increase your knowledge base, but will develop other useful skills which are attractive to employers. Organisational skills, finding information, questioning, varying perspectives, use of resources, computer literacy, understanding statistics, report writing, can all be gained from a degree whatever the subject matter.

City and Guild 7307
For those with an interest in teaching the Certificate in Adult Teaching is a useful tool. Practice in presentation skills can be developed within the job, working with colleagues and parents, but theoretical approaches and alternative styles need to be learned. Also if you wish to pass on your childcare knowledge through courses offered through further education establishments you will probably need to have gained this certificate.

Social work
The professional qualification fo the Diploma in Social Work gives the opportunity to work with children and families in a number of capacities. These can be in residential establishments, special boarding schools, field social work, child protection, day nurseries and other day care provision, and in Scotland – governed by The Children (Scotland) Act 1995 – a unique feature, the Children's Hearing system. Training lasts for two years full time, or its part time equivalent, and is a generic course covering all aspects and age groups.

Speech therapy
If working with children has whetted your appetite to develop language and communication skills maybe speech therapy would interest you. Speech and language therapists are skilled in identifying, assessing and treating communication disorders in children and adults. You would work as a member of the team which may include medical, teaching, and other caring professions. Qualification can be gained through a full-time under graduate degree, or post graduate Diploma or Masters degree.

Satisfaction of childcare

Whether you are a school leaver or already in work, male or female, parent or carer, whatever your area of interest is, you will find a great deal of satisfaction in working with children. It is certainly not an easy option career, it can be physically demanding, mind expanding work, requiring all the skills of management jobs. Working with children is in no way a static profession – there is always more to learn. Keep learning!

Points to remember

- Take the opportunity occasionally for self-assessment, either formally through a training session or seminar, or informally with your manager or friends.

- Do not under-estimate your capabilities, strengths or weaknesses. By being honest you can build on your positives and work on your less positive characteristics.

- Age is no barrier to working with children. If you are a school leaver aim for general child development, play, childcare training as well as experience under supervision. For a mature entrant, perhaps with child rearing experience, gain the general training and look towards any particular area of interest you may have. The opportunities are there, grasp them!

DISCUSSION POINTS

1. How far do you want to go in the childcare profession?

2. Working with children can be mentally and physically exhausting – are you fully prepared for that?

Appendix
National Vocational Qualifications Standards

All NVQs and SVQs are statements of competence which means 'the ability to perform the activities in a job or function to a standard acceptable in employment.'

NVQ IN CHILDCARE AND EDUCATION

Level 2

Core Units

C2 Care for children's physical needs

C4 Support for children's social and emotional development

C6 Contribute to the management of children's behaviour

C8 Set out and clear away play activities

C9 Work with young children

E1 Maintain a child-orientated environment

E2 Maintain the safety of children

P2 Establish and maintain relationships with parents of young children

Endorsements
A Work with babies

B Work in support of others

C Work in a pre-school group

D Work in a community-run pre-school group

NVQ IN CHILDCARE AND EDUCATION

Level 3

Core Units
C2 Care for children's physical needs

C3 Promote the physical development of young children

C5 Promote children's social and emotional development

C7 Provide for the management of children's behaviour

C10 Promote children's sensory and intellectual development

C11 Promote the development of children's language and communication skills

C15 Contribute to the protection of children from abuse

C16 Observe and assess the development and behaviour of children

E1 Maintain a child-oriented environment

E2 Maintain the safety of children

P2 Establish and maintain relationships with parents of young children

Endorsements
A Group care and education

B Family day care

C Pre-school provision

D   Family support

E   Special needs

NVQ IN PLAYWORK

Level 2
D28   Contribute to the planning of a play opportunity

D29   Facilitate a play opportunity to enhance the development of children

D30   Support children's social and emotional development

E7   Contribute to the maintanance and improvement of a child-centred environment

H1   Contribute to the health and safety of self and others

H4   Support the protection of children from abuse

H6   Contribute to children's health and well-being

M3   Contribute to the promotion and improvement of service delivery

P14   Establish and maintain relationships with children and parents

P16   Contribute to the management of children's behaviour

P19   Support the work of a team

NVQ IN PLAYWORK

Level 3
D1   Prepare a programme of activities

D2   Co-ordinate a programme of activities

D25 Prepare play opportunities to enhance children's development

D26 Facilitate play opportunities to enhance children's development

D27 Promote children's social and emotional development

E7 Contribute to the maintenance and improvement of a child-centred environment

H1 Contribute to the health and safety of self and others

H4 Support the protection of children from abuse

H5 Promote children's safety outside the play environment

H6 Contribute to children's health and well-being

IN6 Administer provision

O5 Contribute to the planning, organisation and evaluation of work

P11 Work with colleagues in a team

P14 Establish and maintain relationships with children and parents

P15 Provide for the management of children's behaviour

NVQ IN PLAYWORK DEVELOPMENT

Level 4
E2 Obtain facilities

IN3 Seek, evaluate and organise information for action

IN4 Exchange information to solve problems and make decisions

IN5 Provide specialist advice and information on request

M1 Develop new services to meet the needs of potential clients and customers

M2 Promote and evaluate services to maximise participation

O3 Contribute to the implementation of change in services and systems

P5 Contribute to the recruitment and selection of personnel

P6 Develop teams, individual and self to enhance performance

P8 Create, maintain and enhance effective working relationships

P13 Co-ordinate support to others

R1 Manage and provide physical resources

R5 Develop a new resource

S1 Contribute to the formulation of policy

NVQ IN SPORT AND RECREATION COACHING CHILDREN

Level 3

D1 Prepare a programme of activities

D2 Co-ordinate a programme of activities

D6 Prepare a coaching activity to enhance children's performance

D7 Conduct a coaching activity to enhance children's performance

D8 Prepare an individual training programme to enhance a child's performance

H1 Contribute to the health and safety of self and others

H4 Support the protection of children from abuse

IN4 Exchange information to solve problems and make decisions

IN5 Provide specialist advice and information on request

O5 Contribute to the planning, organisation and evaluation of work

P10 Contribute to the training and development of teams, individuals and self to enhance performance

P11 Work with colleagues in a team

P12 Establish and maintain relationships with organisations and individuals

P13 Co-ordinate support to others

Glossary

Carescheme. Full-day care for school age children in the holidays.
Casual work. Being paid for the hours worked only: no sick or holiday pay or security of contract.
Childcare. Encompasses work in a number of different settings usually relating to under fives or under eights.
Childminding. Looking after children in the carer's own home.
Children Act 1989. Major piece of legislation concerning children's rights and protection.
Crêche. Sessional care for young children, including babies.
CV. Curriculum Vitae: a list of facts which record your professional, academic and personal life relevant to employment.
Equal opportunity. Ensuring no unnecessary barriers are applied to prevent anyone from competing fairly for a post, place, training or chance.
Home Start: Voluntary organisation supporting parents with under five-year-olds.
Kibbutz. Collective farm in Israel where work and childcare is shared amongst members of the community.
Montessori. Nursery and school provision based on teachings of Dr Maria Montessori.
Nannying. Looking after children in the child's own home.
NNEB. National Nursery Examination Board
NVQ/SVQ. National Vocational Qualifications/Scottish Vocational Qualifications.
Opportunity group. Pre-school group catering for disabled children and their non-disabled siblings.
Out-of-school club. Provision for school age children before and after school, in school buildings or elsewhere, while parents work.
Parent and toddler group. Social meeting for parents where

children play, often in same room. Sometimes with supervisors/ activity organisers for children.

Person specification. List of requirements expected for a particular post; used for recruitment purposes.

Playbus. Bus converted into base for play activities.

Playgroup. Usually sessional play experiences for children aged two or three to five years. Can sometimes offer extended days.

Playscheme. Organised play activities in school holidays.

Play therapy. Play, in groups or individually, with sick children.

Playwork. Generally refers to five to 14-year-olds.

Portfolio. Collection of documentation, personal to you, which demonstrates your experiences and training acquired.

Pre-school Learning Alliance. Voluntary organisation supporting pre-school groups. Formerly known as the Pre-school Playgroup Association.

Rakhi. Thread bracelet given by sisters to brothers at Hindu festival of Raksha Bandham.

SCOTVEC. Scottish Vocational Education Council: validating body for awards in Scotland.

Shoppers' crêche. Organised play sessions where children can be left while parents shop.

Special needs. Disabled children and children with learning difficulties or disabilities.

Themed activities. Taking a subject area and designing all activities around that theme *ie* red theme, nature theme, wildlife, clothes.

Toy library. Loaning toys to parents, often on low income or with disabled child, in a similar way to book library loans.

Workplace nursery. Full-day nursery provision provided by employers for their staff.

Further Reading

Bright Ideas – Festivals, Jill Bennett and Archie Millar (Scholastic Publications, 1992).
Convention on the Rights of the Child, United Nations, Switzerland.
Child-Care Employment, Christine Hobart and Jill Frankel (Stanley Thornes, 1996).
The Children Act 1989, Volume 2 Family Support, Day Care and Educational Provision for Young Children, HMSO.
A Curriculum for the Pre-school Child, Audrey M Curtis (NFER-Nelson, 1991).
The Early Years, Iram Siraj-Blatchford (Trentham Books, 1994).
The Equal Opportunities Guide, Phil Clements and Tony Spinks (Kogan Page, 1994).
Good Practice in Playwork, P Bonel and J Linden (Stanley Thornes, 1996).
Guidelines – Good Practice for Full and Extended Daycare Playgroups (Pre-school Playgroups Association, 1993).
How to Become an Au Pair, Mark Hempshell (How To Books Ltd, 1995).
Mamatoto – A Celebration of Birth, The Body Shop Team (Virago, 1991).
Play and Learning for Under Threes (Pre-school Playgroup Association, 1992).
Summer Jobs in Britain, David Woodworth (ed) (Vacation Work, 9 Park End Street, Oxford).
Time to Play – In Early Childhood Education, Tina Bruce (Hodder & Stoughton, 1992).
With Equal Concern, Peter Elfer (ed) (National Children's Bureau, 1995).

Publications
Child Education – monthly
Nursery World – weekly

Useful Addresses

ORGANISATIONS

Au Pair in America,
37 Queens Gate, London SW7 5HR.
Tel: (0171) 581 7311.
Places 18–26-year-olds, with child care experience, for a one year period with families in cities in America. Information pack available.

Business & Technology Education Council (BTEC),
Central House, Upper Woburn Place, London WC1H 0HH.
Tel: (0171) 413 8400.
Validates national qualifications in Early Childhood Studies, Nursery Nursing, and National Vocational Qualifications in Childcare and Education.

The National Childminding Association,
8 Mason's Hill, Bromley, Kent BR2 9EY.
Tel: (0181) 464 6164.
Exists to promote the development of excellence in childminding, and to keep childminders, parents, employers and central and local government informed about best practice.

Council for Awards in Children's Care and Education (CACHE),
8 Chequer Street, St Albans, Hertfordshire AL1 3XZ.
Tel: (01727) 847636.
Enables professional childcare workers gain access to training and assessment in order to provide high quality service to children and families: NNEB, NVQ, ADCE, CCE.

Early Years Trainers Anti-Racist Network (EYTARN),
PO Box 1870, London N12 8JQ.
Focuses particularly on training from an anti-racist perspective. Organises conferences and seminars to consider and promote this stance.

The Equality Learning Centre,
356 Holloway Centre, London N7 6PA.
Tel: (0171) 700 8127.
An information, resource, and development centre for people working with under 8-year-olds. Focusing on all aspects of equality practice including class, gender, culture, race, language, children's rights and disability. Offers training, information services, publications, consultancy, and promotion of toys, books, and other materials.

National Association of Hospital Play Staff,
Thomas Coram Foundation, 40 Brunswick Square, London WC1N 1AZ.
The professional association for workers in this specialist field. Exists to promote high standards of play in hospital, offers support and advice, training and information to members.

The Industrial Society,
Peter Runge House, 3 Carlton House Terrace, London SW1Y 2DG.
Tel: (0171) 839 4300.
Provides consultants and trainers to support industries, including childcare. Presents team building training programmes.

Kids Club Network,
Bellerive House, 3 Muirfield Crescent, London E14 9SZ.
Tel: (0171) 512 2112.
The national organisation promoting and supporting local kids clubs providing play and care before and after school during term time, and all day during the school holidays: KCN Playwork Foundation Course, Investing in Playwork, specialist programmes.

Useful Addresses

London Montessori Centre,
18 Balderton Street, London W1Y 1TG.
Tel: (0171) 493 0165.
Offers a number of full and part-time courses, many of which can be taken by correspondence methods. Accreditation for these courses come from the International Montessori Accreditation of Teachers and Schools (IMATS) council and the Open and Distance Learning Quality Council (ODLQC). Diplomas for range of ages and situations, certificate in nannying, parents' course, BEd (Hons).

The Maria Montessori Training Organisation
26 Lyndhurst Gardens, London NW3 5NW.
Tel: (0171) 435 3646.
Courses are accredited by the Association Montessori Internationale (AMI) where both full and part-time Diploma and Assistant courses are presented. The AMI does not give approval for correspondence courses because of a belief in a tutor guided standard of training. AMI International Diploma, assistants course.

National Children's Bureau
8 Wakley Street, London EC1B 7QE.
Tel: (0171) 843 6041.
  An influential network of childcare professionals and a respected resource of information and expertise. Helps government to formulate policies, produces publications, information packs, has a library and information service, and organises conferences, training and consultations.

National Council for Vocational Qualifications (NCVQ)
222 Euston Road, London NW1 2BZ.
Tel: (0171) 387 9898.
Established by the Government in 1986 to reform and support vocational qualifications.

The National Deaf Children's Society,
15 Dufferin Street, London EC1Y 8PD.
Tel: (0171) 250 0123.
An organisation of families, parents and carers which exists to enable deaf children to maximise their skills and abilities. Offers a range of services throughout the United Kingdom.

National Playbus Association,
93 Whitby Road, Brislington, Bristol BS4 3QF.
Tel: (0117) 977 5375.
A voluntary organisation supporting all forms of playbuses, in their various guises, gaining recognition for their value, producing information, conferences, and giving advice.

Pre-school Learning Alliance,
69 Kings Cross Road, London WC1X 9LL.
Tel: (0171) 833 0991. Helpline: (0171) 837 5513.
Supports voluntary groups offering pre-school provision, provides a variety of nationally recognised courses in most parts of the country. Offers a national telephone helpline for parents and carers seeking guidance on childcare facilities.

Scottish Child Care and Education Board,
6 Kilnford Crescent, Dundonald, Ayrshire KA2 9DW.
Tel: (01563) 850440.
The professional awarding body of Scotland for Preliminary and Registration certificates in Child Care and Education. Details of units and modules taught in colleges, application forms for registration, and clarification on qualifications or combinations of qualifications, can be obtained from the Secretary.

Central Council for the Education and Training of Social Workers (CCETSW)
Information Service, Derbyshire House, St Chad's Street, London WC1H 8AD.
Tel: (0171) 278 2455.
There are also offices in Edinburgh (0131 220 0093), Belfast (01232 665390), and Cardiff (01222 226257). CCETSW is responsible for recognising courses of education and training for work in the personal social services in the UK. Awards qualifications to students successfully completing its courses.

The College of Speech and Language Therapists,
7 Bath Place, Rivington Street, London EC2A 3DR.
Tel: (0171) 613 3855.
Information on speech and language therapy as a career. Leaflets on different areas: work with children, entry requirements,

educational establishments for qualification training, and further information.

The Teacher Training Agency,
Portland House, Stag Place, London SW1E 5TT.
Tel: (01245) 454454.
Information available to make informed choices about teaching as a career. Booklets on training to teach in primary schools, secondary teaching, mature entry including Overseas Trained Teacher Route; information on recent developments in training for teaching. Further addresses available, plus other publications and videos.

Universities and Colleges Admissions Services (UCAS),
PO Box 67, Cheltenham, Gloucestershire GL50 3SH.
The clearing house for degree course entry through which applications should be made.

PUBLICATIONS/ MAGAZINES

Child Education, Villiers House, Clarendon Avenue, Leamington Spa, Warwickshire CV32 5PR.
The Guardian, 119 Farringdon Road, London EC1R 3ER.
The Lady, 39–40 Bedford Street, London WC2E 9ER.
Nursery World, Lector Court, 151–153 Farringdon Road, London EC1R 3AD.

NURSING CAREERS INFORMATION

England
English National Board for Nursing, Midwifery and Health Visiting, Careers Information Centre, PO Box 2EN, London W1A 2EN.

Northern Ireland
The Recruitment Officer, National Board for Nursing, Midwifery and Health Visiting for Northern Ireland, RAC House, 79 Chichester Street, Belfast BT1 4JR.

Scotland
The Nursing Adviser, Scottish Health Service Centre, Crewe Road South, Edinburgh EH4 2LF.

Wales
The Chief Nursing Officer, Welsh Office, Cathays Park, Cardiff CF31 3NQ.

Other health service careers
PO Box 204, London SE99 7UW.

SEASONAL SUMMER/WINTER RESORT WORK

Camp America,
37a Queen's Gate, London SW7 5HR.
Tel: (0171) 581 7373.
Recruits to American summer camps and families to spend nine weeks passing on skills to children of all ages and abilities. Variety of opportunities available – counsellors for special needs camps, Christian and Jewish camps, Scout and Guide camps; also qualified nurses as infirmary assistants, and family companions.

Esprit Holidays Ltd,
Oaklands, Reading Road North, Fleet, Hampshire GU13 8AA.
Tel: (01252) 625177.
Qualified nannies for chalet nurseries and Snow Clubs for three to ten-year-olds required from December to April/May. Limited number of nannies employed June to September.

Mark Warner
20 Kensington Church Street, London W8 4EP.
A travel company specialising in summer beach club and winter sport holidays employing staff in a variety of capacities including nannies and childcare managers.

PGL Travel Ltd,
Alton Court, Penyard Lane, Ross-on-Wye, Herefordshire, HR9 5NR.
Tel: (01989) 767300.
Activity holidays for children in 24 locations in the UK and France. Selects staff on basis of activity qualifications or experience,

previous work with children, entertainment and/or management skills. Travel couriers accompany children by coach or rail from pick-up points around the country to PGL centres.

Pontin's Holiday Club,
PO Box 100, Sagar House, The Green, Eccleston, Chorley, Lancashire PR7 5QQ.
Tel: (01257) 452452.
If you are prepared to work hard during a six day week, are able to mix with people of all ages, prepared to work flexible hours, able to use your initiative, and can relate to children, seasonal jobs are available in the UK. Arranging competitions, games, swimming galas, sports days, outings, clubs, entertainment.

OTHER OPPORTUNITIES

British Airways Plc,
Marketing Resourcing (CSA), Assessment and Selection, Meadowbank, PO Box 59, Hounslow TW5 9QX.
The opportunity to take responsibility to care for unaccompanied children and young people between flights, to and from aircraft, and other relevant duties.

Disney Cruise Lines,
210 Celebration Place, Suite 400, Celebration, FL34747 4600, USA.
Due to start a cruise programme in 1998. With its emphasis on the child, children's decks and facilities, and promising to be the first vessels properly geared up for the young customers, opportunities will exist for suitably qualified staff with childcare and play backgrounds.

P & O Cruises,
Richmond House, Terminus Terrace, Southampton SO14 3PN.
Tel: (01703) 534200.
Suitably qualified staff required to work with children between two and 17 years. Requires extensive experience of childcare or play work. Relevant qualifications include NNEB, Teaching Certificate, PLA Diploma, NVQ Childcare and Education or Playwork at Level 3, Kids Club Network Diploma, or Youth and Community Work Qualification.

Index

Acceptable words/unacceptable words, 31
Activity holidays, 54
ADCE, 75
Advertisements, 83–84
Affecting benefits, 24
All year round provision, 22
Application letter, 87
Attending training, 75

Bi-lingual courses, 74
BTEC, 70

CACHE, 69
Camps in America, 53
Carescheme, 48
Caring in leisure facilities, 60
Casual work, 28
Celebrating festivals, 34
Child friendly cities, 58
Childminding, 40, 73
Children Act 1989, 68
Children's and family centres, 38
Choosing a course, 69
City and Guilds 7307, 119
Coaching children, 60
Combined centres, 55
Convincing yourself, 16
Cooking with the children, 34
Correspondence courses, 76
Counselling/advice, 103
Crêche, 39
Curriculum Vitae, 87

Day nursery, 37
Degrees, 118
Developing relationships, 106
Developing specialisms, 114
Disabled children, 45
Disabled people, 108

Early years teaching, 55
Environmental play, 64
Equal opportunities, 84
Experience versus pay, 23

Family responsibility, 14
Fitting in with school hours, 21
Further training, 110

Giving yourself confidence, 16

Helping at school, 31
Home Start, 32
Hospital playwork, 73
Hospital schools, 44
Hospital work and health care, 43

Ideas for themes, 64
Identifying your strengths, 16
In-service training, 109
Integrated provision, 45
Interview decisions, 102
Interviews, 96
Interview – step by step guide, 103
Interview questions, 102

Index

Job description, 91
Jobs in school hours, 21
Jobs outside of school time, 21

Kibbutz, 54

Leisure activities, 48
Listening bus, 67
Local Authority provision, 37
Local initiatives, 62
Looking for childcare, 21

Maternity and baby care, 44
Management, 111
Mobile crêches, 63
Montessori courses, 72
Montessori provision, 46

Nannying, 40
NNEB, 69
NVQ assessor, 118
NVQ/SVQ, 77

Ofsted Inspector, 118
Opportunity group, 30
Other training opportunities, 80
Out-of-school clubs, 47

Parent and toddler group, 27
Parent helper, 28
Personal development, 35
Person specification, 91
Playbuses, 66
Playgroup, 28, 42
Playschemes, 51
Play therapy, 43
Playwork training, 73
Portfolio, 78, 81
Practicalities from home, 18
Practising your skills, 108
Pre-interview preparations, 98
Pre-school Learning Alliance, 71
Previous work experience, 18
Primary school, 51
Private sector, 38

Providing for employees, 49

Qualifications, 68

Rounding your skills, 118

Scottish Child Care and
    Education Board, 70
Seeking advice, 68
Sharing families, 40
Sharing your culture, 34
Sharing your lifestyle, 34
Shoppers' crêche, 57
Ski slopes, 53
Social work, 119
Social work aspects, 39
Speech therapy, 119
Special events, 62
Specialisms – developing them,
    114
Specialist groups, 48
Special needs children, 45
Sports activities, 35
Starting with a little, 24
Straight from school, 13
Sunday school, 35
SVQ/NVQ, 77

Taking advantage of
    opportunities, 26
Taking your children, 20
Teaching, 55
Terminology, 31
Themed sessions, 64
Training, 68

Unacceptable words/acceptable
    words, 31

Voluntary work, 27

Weighing up the pros and cons,
    22
What is the potential?, 24
Workplace nursery, 38

PASSING THAT INTERVIEW
Your step-by-step guide to achieving success

Judith Johnstone

Everyone knows how to shine at interview – or do they? When every candidate becomes the perfect clone of the one before, you have to have that extra 'something' to raise your chances above the rest. Using a systematic and practical approach, this How To book takes you step-by-step through the essential pre-interview groundwork, the interview encounter itself, and what you can learn from the experience afterwards. The book contains sample pre- and post-interview correspondence, and is complete with a guide to further reading, glossary of terms, and index. 'This is from the first class How To Books stable.' *Escape Committee Newsletter*. 'Offers a fresh approach to a well documented subject.' *Newscheck/Careers Service Bulletin*. 'A complete step-by-step guide.' *The Association of Business Executives*. Judith Johnstone is a Graduate of the Institute of Personnel & Development; she has been an instructor in Business Studies and adult literacy tutor, and has long experience of helping people at work.

144pp. illus. 1 85703 360 4. 4th edition.

HOW TO BECOME AN AU PAIR
Your guide to employment opportunities worldwide

Mark Hempshell

There are thousands of vacancies waiting to be filled each year for au pair work and other domestic employment, and the work often means the chance to travel and live abroad in exotic locations. Step-by-step, this book explains the work involved, the personal qualities required, where to locate the vacancies, how to apply and how to negotiate your job offer, how to cope with language and cultural difficulties, and how to cope with all the practicalities of your first assignment. Complete with real life case histories, guide to employment agencies, newspaper job ads including overseas, and country-by-country guide to au pairing worldwide. Mark Hempshell is a specialist writer on international employment topics.

144pp. illus. 1 85703 120 2.

GETTING THAT JOB
The complete job finders handbook

Joan Fletcher

Now in its fourth edition this popular book provides a clear step-by-step guide to identifying job opportunities, writing successful application letters, preparing for interviews and being selected. 'A valuable book.' *Teachers Weekly*. 'Cheerful and appropriate . . . particularly helpful in providing checklists designed to bring system to searching for a job. This relaxed, friendly and very helpful little book could bring lasting benefit.' *Times Educational Supplement*. 'Clear and concise . . . should be mandatory reading by all trainees.' *Comlon Magazine (LCCI)*. Joan Fletcher is an experienced Manager and Student Counsellor.

112pp. illus. 1 85703 380 9. 4th edition.

CAREER NETWORKING
How to develop the right contacts to help you throughout your working life

Laurel Alexander

Unemployed? Redundant? Wanting promotion?— then career networking is for you. By systematically networking with other people, you can build bridges which could bring in offers of work. This book helps you take control of your working life through setting goals, assessing your networking needs and cultivating a supportive network. By working step-by-step through each practical chapter, you will understand how you can develop and plan your career through other people. Discover how you can be seen as a specialist selling something everyone wants using effective communication skills, assertive behaviour and being seen as a positive person. Learn how to network a room, how to gather information anywhere, from anyone. Do you know how to network using E-mail, the Internet and other technology? This book tells you how. There is further information on starting your own network, getting on other people's networks and extending your network. Laurel Alexander is a freelance trainer and consultant in career development and has helped many individuals improve their working life. She is author of *Surviving Redundancy* in this series.

136pp. illus. 1 85703 350 7.

HOW TO START A NEW CAREER
Managing a better future for yourself

Judith Johnstone

More people than ever before are faced with big career changes today. Few if any jobs are 'for life'. Now in its second edition, this How To book helps you manage your entry into a new career effectively. It is aimed at anyone making a new start, whatever his or her age or background. It looks at who you are and what you are. It helps you evaluate your life skills, to recognise which careers you should concentrate on, and how to make a realistic plan for a happy and productive future. 'Written very much in the style of a work book, with practical exercises and pro formas for the student to complete . . . Well written—would be a useful addition to the library of any guidance practitioner working with adults.' *Newscheck/Careers Service Bulletin.*

140pp. illus. 1 85703 139 3. 2nd edition.

GETTING YOUR FIRST JOB
How to win the offer of good prospects and a regular pay packet

Penny Hitchin

It's a tough world for jobhunters—especially for those with no track record. The days when newcomers to the job market could walk into 'A job for life' have gone. Jobseekers today must impress a potential employer with their personal qualities and attitudes as well as their paper qualifications. Once in work, they must show themselves to be willing, adaptable and flexible—able to learn new skills quickly and cope with constant change. This readable handbook offers young people a real insight into what employers are looking for, encouraging the reader to take a constructive and positive approach to finding their first job. The book includes lots of practical examples, self-assessment material and typical case studies. Penny Hitchin has run Jobfinder programmes and written careers books and materials for TV and radio campaigns on training and employment.

160pp. illus. 1 85703 300 0.

How To Books

How To Books provide practical help on a large range of topics. They are available through all good bookshops or can be ordered direct from the distributors. Just tick the titles you want and complete the form on the following page.

- Apply to an Industrial Tribunal (£7.99)
- Applying for a Job (£8.99)
- Applying for a United States Visa (£15.99)
- Backpacking Round Europe (£8.99)
- Be a Freelance Journalist (£8.99)
- Be a Freelance Secretary (£8.99)
- Become a Freelance Sales Agent (£9.99)
- Become an Au Pair (£8.99)
- Becoming a Father (£8.99)
- Buy & Run a Shop (£8.99)
- Buy & Run a Small Hotel (£8.99)
- Buying a Personal Computer (£9.99)
- Career Networking (£8.99)
- Career Planning for Women (£8.99)
- Cash from your Computer (£9.99)
- Choosing a Nursing Home (£9.99)
- Choosing a Package Holiday (£8.99)
- Claim State Benefits (£9.99)
- Collecting a Debt (£9.99)
- Communicate at Work (£7.99)
- Conduct Staff Appraisals (£7.99)
- Conducting Effective Interviews (£8.99)
- Coping with Self Assessment (£9.99)
- Copyright & Law for Writers (£8.99)
- Counsel People at Work (£7.99)
- Creating a Twist in the Tale (£8.99)
- Creative Writing (£9.99)
- Critical Thinking for Students (£8.99)
- Dealing with a Death in the Family (£9.99)
- Do Voluntary Work Abroad (£8.99)
- Do Your Own Advertising (£8.99)
- Do Your Own PR (£8.99)
- Doing Business Abroad (£10.99)
- Doing Business on the Internet (£12.99)
- Emigrate (£9.99)
- Employ & Manage Staff (£8.99)
- Find Temporary Work Abroad (£8.99)
- Finding a Job in Canada (£9.99)
- Finding a Job in Computers (£8.99)
- Finding a Job in New Zealand (£9.99)
- Finding a Job with a Future (£8.99)
- Finding Work Overseas (£9.99)
- Freelance DJ-ing (£8.99)
- Freelance Teaching & Tutoring (£9.99)
- Get a Job Abroad (£10.99)
- Get a Job in America (£9.99)
- Get a Job in Australia (£9.99)
- Get a Job in Europe (£9.99)
- Get a Job in France (£9.99)
- Get a Job in Travel & Tourism (£8.99)
- Get into Radio (£8.99)
- Getting into Films & Television (£10.99)
- Getting That Job (£8.99)
- Getting your First Job (£8.99)
- Going to University (£8.99)
- Helping your Child to Read (£8.99)
- How to Study & Learn (£8.99)
- Investing in People (£9.99)
- Investing in Stocks & Shares (£9.99)
- Keep Business Accounts (£7.99)
- Know Your Rights at Work (£8.99)
- Live & Work in America (£9.99)
- Live & Work in Australia (£12.99)
- Live & Work in Germany (£9.99)
- Live & Work in Greece (£9.99)
- Live & Work in Italy (£8.99)
- Live & Work in New Zealand (£9.99)
- Live & Work in Portugal (£9.99)
- Live & Work in the Gulf (£9.99)
- Living & Working in Britain (£8.99)
- Living & Working in China (£9.99)
- Living & Working in Hong Kong (£10.99)
- Living & Working in Israel (£10.99)
- Living & Working in Saudi Arabia (£12.99)
- Living & Working in the Netherlands (£9.99)
- Making a Complaint (£8.99)
- Making a Wedding Speech (£8.99)
- Manage a Sales Team (£8.99)
- Manage an Office (£8.99)
- Manage Computers at Work (£8.99)
- Manage People at Work (£8.99)
- Manage Your Career (£8.99)
- Managing Budgets & Cash Flows (£9.99)
- Managing Meetings (£8.99)
- Managing Your Personal Finances (£8.99)
- Managing Yourself (£8.99)
- Market Yourself (£8.99)
- Master Book-Keeping (£8.99)
- Mastering Business English (£8.99)
- Master GCSE Accounts (£8.99)
- Master Public Speaking (£8.99)
- Migrating to Canada (£12.99)
- Obtaining Visas & Work Permits (£9.99)
- Organising Effective Training (£9.99)
- Pass Exams Without Anxiety (£7.99)
- Passing That Interview (£8.99)
- Plan a Wedding (£7.99)
- Planning Your Gap Year (£8.99)
- Prepare a Business Plan (£8.99)
- Publish a Book (£9.99)
- Publish a Newsletter (£9.99)
- Raise Funds & Sponsorship (£7.99)
- Rent & Buy Property in France (£9.99)
- Rent & Buy Property in Italy (£9.99)

How To Books

___ Research Methods (£8.99)
___ Retire Abroad (£8.99)
___ Return to Work (£7.99)
___ Run a Voluntary Group (£8.99)
___ Setting up Home in Florida (£9.99)
___ Spending a Year Abroad (£8.99)
___ Start a Business from Home (£7.99)
___ Start a New Career (£6.99)
___ Starting to Manage (£8.99)
___ Starting to Write (£8.99)
___ Start Word Processing (£8.99)
___ Start Your Own Business (£8.99)
___ Study Abroad (£8.99)
___ Study & Live in Britain (£7.99)
___ Studying at University (£8.99)
___ Studying for a Degree (£8.99)
___ Successful Grandparenting (£8.99)
___ Successful Mail Order Marketing (£9.99)
___ Successful Single Parenting (£8.99)
___ Survive Divorce (£8.99)
___ Surviving Redundancy (£8.99)
___ Taking in Students (£8.99)
___ Taking on Staff (£8.99)
___ Taking Your A-Levels (£8.99)
___ Teach Abroad (£8.99)
___ Teach Adults (£8.99)
___ Teaching Someone to Drive (£8.99)
___ Travel Round the World (£8.99)
___ Understand Finance at Work (£8.99)
___ Use a Library (£7.99)

___ Use the Internet (£9.99)
___ Winning Consumer Competitions (£8.99)
___ Winning Presentations (£8.99)
___ Work from Home (£8.99)
___ Work in an Office (£7.99)
___ Work in Retail (£8.99)
___ Work with Dogs (£8.99)
___ Working Abroad (£14.99)
___ Working as a Holiday Rep (£9.99)
___ Working in Japan (£10.99)
___ Working in Photography (£8.99)
___ Working in the Gulf (£10.99)
___ Working in Hotels & Catering (£9.99)
___ Working on Contract Worldwide (£9.99)
___ Working on Cruise Ships (£9.99)
___ Write a Press Release (£9.99)
___ Write a Report (£8.99)
___ Write an Assignment (£8.99)
___ Write & Sell Computer Software (£9.99)
___ Write for Publication (£8.99)
___ Write for Television (£8.99)
___ Writing a CV that Works (£8.99)
___ Writing a Non Fiction Book (£9.99)
___ Writing an Essay (£8.99)
___ Writing & Publishing Poetry (£9.99)
___ Writing & Selling a Novel (£8.99)
___ Writing Business Letters (£8.99)
___ Writing Reviews (£9.99)
___ Writing Your Dissertation (£8.99)

To: Plymbridge Distributors Ltd, Plymbridge House, Estover Road, Plymouth PL6 7PZ.
Customer Services Tel: (01752) 202301. Fax: (01752) 202331.

Please send me copies of the titles I have indicated. Please add postage & packing (UK £1, Europe including Eire, £2, World £3 airmail).

☐ I enclose cheque/PO payable to Plymbridge Distributors Ltd for £ _____

☐ Please charge to my ☐ MasterCard, ☐ Visa, ☐ AMEX card.

Account No. ☐☐☐☐☐☐☐☐☐☐☐☐☐☐☐☐

Card Expiry Date ☐☐ 19 ☎ **Credit Card orders may be faxed or phoned.**

Customer Name (CAPITALS) ....

Address ....

.... Postcode ....

Telephone .... Signature ....

Every effort will be made to despatch your copy as soon as possible but to avoid possible disappointment please allow up to 21 days for despatch time (42 days if overseas). Prices and availability are subject to change without notice.

Code BPA